Airline Revenue Management

Curt Cramer · Andreas Thams

Airline Revenue Management

Current Practices and Future Directions

Curt Cramer
Mannheim, Baden-Württemberg
Germany

Andreas Thams
University of Applied Sciences Worms
Hamburg, Germany

ISBN 978-3-658-33720-9   ISBN 978-3-658-33721-6 (eBook)
https://doi.org/10.1007/978-3-658-33721-6

© Springer Fachmedien Wiesbaden GmbH, part of Springer Nature 2021
This work is subject to copyright. All rights are reserved by the Publisher, whether the whole or part of the material is concerned, specifically the rights of translation, reprinting, reuse of illustrations, recitation, broadcasting, reproduction on microfilms or in any other physical way, and transmission or information storage and retrieval, electronic adaptation, computer software, or by similar or dissimilar methodology now known or hereafter developed.
The use of general descriptive names, registered names, trademarks, service marks, etc. in this publication does not imply, even in the absence of a specific statement, that such names are exempt from the relevant protective laws and regulations and therefore free for general use.
The publisher, the authors, and the editors are safe to assume that the advice and information in this book are believed to be true and accurate at the date of publication. Neither the publisher nor the authors or the editors give a warranty, expressed or implied, with respect to the material contained herein or for any errors or omissions that may have been made. The publisher remains neutral with regard to jurisdictional claims in published maps and institutional affiliations.

This Springer Gabler imprint is published by the registered company Springer Fachmedien Wiesbaden GmbH part of Springer Nature.
The registered company address is: Abraham-Lincoln-Str. 46, 65189 Wiesbaden, Germany

Preface

Preface by Curt Cramer

When Andreas Thams and I met five years ago while becoming members of the senior management team at a tourism firm, we quickly discovered our shared passion: data science. With both of us having a mathematical background and applied experience in creating business value through data science—Andreas in revenue management functions at airlines and myself as a top management consultant in various industries like media and wholesale—we immediately saw huge potential in applying these methodologies to various parts of the firm.

Fast forward to today and the field of data science has evolved even further, not only from a methodology and technology point of view, but especially considering its acceptance and its degree of adoption. It undoubtedly still is a field that is not self-explanatory and that requires a certain degree of skill, experience, and understanding to implement.

But having worked in this field for 20 years, starting in academia and now for over 10 years professionally, including senior management roles for data science functions at a major consultancy as well as Europe's largest retailer, the contrast between then and now could not be any stronger: through the digital nature of our lives, data are being generated in abundance. Powerful resources to process these data volumes and compute analytical models are literally seconds and cents away when 20 years ago we had to wait weeks for procurement and installation, all after a large initial capital outlay. Also, methodologies have evolved and been made accessible through software libraries like scikit-learn, Keras, and fast.ai that abstract away any details unnecessary for practical applications.

It is at this point in time that Andreas and I decided to make our humble contribution to further removing part of the mystery surrounding data science. In this monograph, the reader is introduced to the area of airline revenue management from a modern perspective, followed by an up-to-date course on data science that is heavily inspired by our business experience in this field.

The data science course introduces the most relevant methodologies and terminologies and provides a framework for defining and approaching business problems with data science. To give a complete context, it also discusses related IT concepts ("big data") and the question of how to embed data science organizationally. Furthermore, it makes the methodological concepts tangible through worked examples from the area of revenue management. The concise nature of this course does not do justice to the broad scope of data science which is why we also provide the reader with an extensive annotated bibliography of books that we found to provide the best in-depth reading on theoretical, practical, and applied aspects.

We hope that the reader will gather enough from this course to be in a better position for setting up and driving data science initiatives thereafter. Even more so, we would like to rekindle the interest of readers who had a previous educational exposure to the topic, but did not have the time for a modern introduction into data science. Now is the best time to consider data science because I am certain about one thing: of all topics hyped under the label of digitalization, data science (and the closely linked cloud platform technologies) is foundational and is here to stay.

Preface by Andreas Thams

Revenue management has a long tradition in the airline and travel industry and has become an integral part of commercial organizations in nearly all large and medium-sized companies. The foundations of classical revenue management have been laid in the 1970s, when the availability of data was limited, the distribution landscape was characterized by pure B2B sales, and the terminology of data science was only known to an expert audience. Since then, the sales and marketing approach of many companies in the industry has substantially changed, focusing on a higher share of direct distribution through their online distribution channels. Beyond the potentially lower distribution costs, which are typically associated with direct sales, their distribution channels also offer the opportunity to collect data about customer behavior and preferences. This allows sales and marketing organizations to better understand the actual needs of customers by recognizing certain demand patterns in almost real time.

Throughout the first part, this book explains and describes the basic approaches, steps, and methodologies of classical revenue management from an airline perspective. Each section is enriched by practical experiences and insights Curt and I gained during our time as managers and consultants at different companies. The content is perfectly suitable for practitioners, who want to extend or renew their knowledge in the field of airline revenue management, as well as for students and scientists, who want to gain insights into airline revenue management from a uniquely combined theoretical and practical perspective.

While we have seen a tremendous and continuous change of sales and marketing processes and approaches since the late 1990s, as described above, revenue management has not experienced a major transformation levering the full potential of customer-centric data. Instead, classical revenue management techniques are still the working horse of topline optimization of airlines. For this reason, the second part of the book gives an introduction and outlook into the potentials arising from data science.

By offering different views and perspectives on airline revenue management, the book intends to close a part of the existing gap in the literature offering a consistent picture on current and future paths in this area.

Mannheim, Germany Curt Cramer
Hamburg, Germany Andreas Thams
January 2021

Contents

1 Fundamentals of Airline Revenue Management 1
   1.1 Prerequisites for Applying Revenue Management 1
   1.2 The Rationale for Applying Revenue Management 4
   1.3 Fundamental KPIs Used in Airline Revenue Management 6
   1.4 Practitioner View: Balancing Yield and Load Factor 8
   1.5 Revenue Management Within the Value Chain of an Airline 10
   1.6 Challenge: Seasonality of Demand 10
   1.7 Demand Curve Revisited 11
   1.8 Checkpoint Chap. 1 12

2 Computerized Revenue Management 15
   2.1 Process Flow of a Revenue Management System 15
   2.2 Limitations of Fully Automated Revenue Management 18
   2.3 Checkpoint Chap. 2 20

3 Estimation and Forecasting 21
   3.1 Practical Relevance of Estimation and Forecasting 21
   3.2 Unconstraining of Demand Data: EM Algorithm 24
   3.3 Pick-up Forecasting 30
   3.4 Stationary and Nonstationary Time-Series Models 32
   3.5 ARMA Processes 33
   3.6 M-period Moving Average Forecasting 35
   3.7 Exponential Smoothing 36
   3.8 Checkpoint Chap. 3 37

4 Optimization, Types of Control, and Overbooking 39
   4.1 Booking Limits 39
   4.2 Littlewood's Rule 41
   4.3 Expected Marginal Seat Revenue (EMSR) 43
   4.4 Overbooking 45
   4.5 Rationale for Overbooking 45
   4.6 Deterministic Overbooking Approach 47

	4.7	Stochastic Overbooking Approach	48
	4.8	Cost-based Overbooking Approach	49
	4.9	Legal Implications: EU Regulation 261	50
	4.10	Checkpoint Chap. 4	51

5 Network Revenue Management 53
5.1	Pros and Cons of Network Revenue Management	53
5.2	The Fundamentals of Network Revenue Management	54
5.3	Revenue Value Buckets	56
5.4	Displacement Costs	57
5.5	Bid Price Control	58
5.6	Checkpoint Chap. 5	58

6 Ancillary Revenues 61
6.1	Types of Ancillary Products	64
6.2	Implications for Revenue Management	65
6.3	Checkpoint Chap. 6	67

7 Data Science and Revenue Management 71
7.1	The Fundamental Idea(s) Behind Data Science	72
	7.1.1 Understanding Analytics: Model-based Analytical Approaches	72
	7.1.2 Applying Analytics: A Taxonomy of Modern Analytical Methods	74
	7.1.2.1 Statistics	75
	7.1.2.2 Mathematical Optimization	76
	7.1.2.3 Machine Learning	77
	7.1.3 The Analytical Cycle: Solving Business Problems with Analytical Methods	78
7.2	Engineering Analytics: Big Data Infrastructure and Data Pipelines	80
7.3	Managing Analytics: Structuring Analytical Capabilities and Processes	81
7.4	Data Science—Revenue Management Use Cases	84
	7.4.1 Data Science—Use Case: Mid-/long-term Demand Forecasting	85
	7.4.1.1 Business Problem	85
	7.4.1.2 Data Sourcing and Structure	85
	7.4.1.3 Methodological Problem	89
	7.4.1.4 Goal Definition	91
	7.4.1.5 Development of the Approach(es)	95
	7.4.1.6 Results and Discussion	105

	7.4.2	Data Science: Use Case—Overbooking	107
		7.4.2.1 Business Problem	107
		7.4.2.2 Data Sourcing and Structure	107
		7.4.2.3 Methodological Problem and Goal Definition	107
		7.4.2.4 Development of the Approach(es)	107
		7.4.2.5 Results and Discussion	108
7.5	Data Science—An Annotated Bibliography		108
	7.5.1	Theory	109
	7.5.2	Practical	110
	7.5.3	Applied	111
7.6	Checkpoint Chap. 7		111

Bibliography 113

List of Figures

Fig. 1.1	Major steps in revenue management and relevant KPIs	3
Fig. 1.2	Overview of prerequisites for applying revenue management	4
Fig. 1.3	Different customer segments have demand for a limited number of seats on a certain flight	5
Fig. 1.4	Price-quantity curve for hypothetical example flight	7
Fig. 1.5	RASK and CASK development, Air Berlin PLC, 2012–2016	8
Fig. 1.6	The most important ingredients affecting the overall revenue management strategy	9
Fig. 1.7	Schematic commercial value chain of an airline	10
Fig. 1.8	Schematic seasonality pattern of an airline	11
Fig. 1.9	Demand curve with additional price points	12
Fig. 2.1	General process flow of a revenue management system	16
Fig. 2.2	Schematic overview of a revenue management system	17
Fig. 2.3	Example for simple rule-based revenue management	20
Fig. 3.1	Booking curve for a single flight event, current year versus previous year	23
Fig. 3.2	Cumulative observed demand per booking class on a single route	23
Fig. 3.3	Schematic process flow of a revenue management system including unconstraining of demand data	25
Fig. 3.4	Histogram for true Y as generated from R code	28
Fig. 3.5	Likelihood function for Y_{obs} dependent on the underlying mean of the normal distribution	30
Fig. 3.6	Behavior of an AR(1) process for different values of α	34
Fig. 3.7	Forecasting with exponential smoothing using example data with $\alpha = 0.5$	37
Fig. 4.1	Example of partitioned and nested booking classes	41
Fig. 4.2	Application of EMSR-a to determine the optimal set of controls in a two-class environment	44
Fig. 4.3	EMSR-a extended to three booking classes	45
Fig. 4.4	Graphical representation of the cost-based overbooking approach	50

Fig. 5.1	Schematic overview of a hub-and-spoke network with New York and Zurich as hub airports	54
Fig. 5.2	Las Vegas to Zurich as an example of a simple O&D problem	55
Fig. 6.1	Total ancillary revenue in the airline industry from 2011 to 2020 (in billion U.S. dollars). (Source: Statista / Ideaworks)	62
Fig. 6.2	Return on invested capital by region, 2004–2011. (Source: IATA 2013)	63
Fig. 6.3	Airlines with the highest ancillary revenue as a share of total revenue in 2019, source: IdeaWorks	63
Fig. 6.4	Schematic categorization of ancillary revenue sources	66
Fig. 6.5	Schematic revenue generation from product up-sell opportunities throughout the customer journey	67
Fig. 6.6	Product specification by fare type, Ryanair, April 2020. (Source: Own analysis / www.ryanair.com)	68
Fig. 7.1	Conceptual diagram of a mathematical model of a real situation (see Kaiser, G., & Stender, P. (2013). Complex modelling problems in co-operative, self-directed learning environments. In G. Stillman, G. Kaiser, W. Blum, & J. Brown (Eds.), *Teaching mathematical modelling: Connecting to research and practice* (pp. 277–293). Dordrecht: Springer)	73
Fig. 7.2	CRISP-DM, the cross-industry standard process for data mining (this depiction (C) Kenneth Jensen)	79
Fig. 7.3	Structure of data pipelines	82
Fig. 7.4	Conversion of xls to xlsx format prior to openpyxl import	87
Fig. 7.5	STL decomposition of the PAX FRA-MUC traveled time series	90
Fig. 7.6	Naïve forecast example	92
Fig. 7.7	Seasonal naïve forecast example	93
Fig. 7.8	Naive forecasting error (MAPE)	94
Fig. 7.9	Seasonal naive forecasting error (MAPE)	95
Fig. 7.10	Forecast error (MAPE) as a function of the number of features k in a linear regression model with RFE(k)	101
Fig. 7.11	Forecasting performance of the linear regression model with RFE	101
Fig. 7.12	Forecasting performance of the ensemble model	102
Fig. 7.13	Forecasting performance (MAPE) as a function of the network capacity	104
Fig. 7.14	Seasonal naive forecasting error (MAPE)	105
Fig. 7.15	Ensemble forecasting error (MAPE)	106

List of Tables

Table 1.1	Assumed willingness to pay and demand per customer type for hypothetical example flight	6
Table 3.1	Applying pick-up forecasting to an artificial example dataset	31
Table 4.1	Denied boarding by marketing carrier, scheduled domestic flights, and international flights originating in the U.S., July–September 2019	48
Table 5.1	Revenue buckets derived from virtual class mapping	57
Table 6.1	Worldwide airline financial results per departing passenger, USD, 2012	64

Fundamentals of Airline Revenue Management

While unit revenues have become constantly under pressure throughout the entire travel industry in the last decades, revenue management has become an integral and decisive part of a commercial airline organization. Technical and organizational strengths and weaknesses in this field usually directly translate into competitive advantages and disadvantages associated with an immediate rise or decline in the profitability of an airline. In extreme cases, a continuous underinvestment into revenue management systems, approaches, and organizations may even bring an entire company into severe difficulties. Some of the recent airline insolvencies have a least been accelerated to some extent by misaligned processes in revenue management in combination with high manual workloads as a result of little or small investments into modern revenue management solutions. Hence, more than ever before revenue management is a decisive lever for the commercial performance of an airline. Technological innovations and a constant change of airline business models toward selling ancillary services and retailing will further increase the relevance but also the challenges for revenue management professionals.

Throughout this chapter, we are going to bring current developments in airline revenue management into a wider perspective and highlight the fundamental idea and basic mechanisms of revenue management.

1.1 Prerequisites for Applying Revenue Management

The first main ingredient for modern revenue management is the availability of transparent and reliable data. This might sound trivial, but in practice, even large organizations tend to have challenges with providing the data needed for effective revenue management. Typically, when introducing a modern revenue management solution, a substantial part of the project work will be dedicated to data sourcing and data quality management, particularly in the first phase of an implementation project. This includes the detection of structural breaks and outliers in the underlying historical dataset.[1] Fundamental changes in the competitive environment, e.g., market entry or exit of a competitor, or operational disruptions are events, which might lead to biased results from the revenue management workflow.

Revenue management consists of three major steps:

1. Data sourcing
2. Forecasting
3. Optimization

Figure 1.1 depicts these steps as the core part of revenue management and relates them to relevant commercial key performance indicators (KPIs). The gray area represents the variables of interest for the revenue management analyst. Throughout the course of this book, we will further elaborate on some of these KPIs, including their relevance and meaning.

In general, the application of revenue management requires certain product characteristics to be fulfilled. In the following, we will list these requirements and explain each of them briefly. If a product does not meet all of these characteristics, it will be not suitable for applying revenue management techniques. Or to put it differently, any product fulfilling these requirements will be suited for revenue management approaches, as outlined in this book.

1. **Fixed capacity**: the capacity to be marketed and sold is known and fixed and does not change over time. In theory, this sounds quite simple, but in practice, we often find situations where this prerequisite is violated. Aircraft type changes are probably the most frequent cases, where over time capacity does not remain steady and changes during the booking period. This has an immediate and substantial impact on the effectiveness of revenue management, as forecasts tend to be biased, as they rely on historical data. Furthermore, the results of the optimization step will be suboptimal, as either too much or too little capacity has been on sale. Changing the seating capacity from a narrow to a wide-body aircraft just a few weeks before the departure of a flight will naturally mean that the steering and marketing approach until that point of time has been built on the wrong assumptions. Hence, fixed capacity is required for applying revenue management techniques, which we will present in the following.
2. **Product is perishable**: opposite to other goods and services, a flight seat is perishable. After check-in has been closed, the flight/product is gone. The same is true for other

---

[1] As this point, we will not discuss the potential impacts of the COVID-19 pandemic on data consistency. Nonetheless, the reader needs to be aware that demand patterns and data characteristics before and after the crisis might significantly differ constituting a remarkable challenge from the perspective of revenue management.

1.1 Prerequisites for Applying Revenue Management

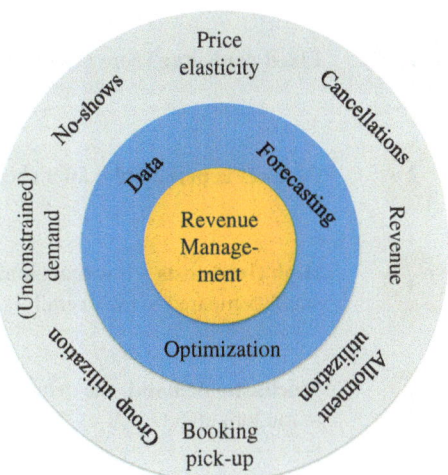

Fig. 1.1 Major steps in revenue management and relevant KPIs

products in the travel industry like hotel beds, cruises, or even concerts and sports events. If this assumption would not be fulfilled, sales could go on forever, until the product is finally sold or sold out. Products such as furniture or cell phones typically violate this requirement, which means that they are not suited for revenue management.

3. **High fixed costs—low marginal costs**: the costs of an additional passenger are small compared to the overall fixed costs of a flight. This assumption allows us to talk about *revenue* management, where costs are theoretically completely out of scope. In reality, of course, costs do matter, particularly when it comes to pricing. The lower end of the price interval is basically defined by variable costs per passenger, which can be significant at some major international airports like Frankfurt, Amsterdam, or London-Heathrow. In practice, the commercial area, which includes revenue management and pricing, will align the pricing structure initially with finance and controlling to make sure that the planned and budgeted level of profit will be achievable with the topline performance resulting from the intended and planned revenue management and pricing approach.
4. **Stochastic demand**: the demand for each flight differs and is subject to unforeseeable random effects. If future demand would be deterministic and foreseeable, revenue management would be obsolete, as capacity allocations would be entirely plannable and static.
5. **Advance bookings**: revenue management requires that bookings are possible in advance. This assumption holds for a wide range of products in the travel industry such as flights, hotels, cruises, etc.

Figure 1.2 summarizes the five prerequisites for revenue management in a comprehensive overview. Furthermore, we shortly state the background and rationale for each of the five items.

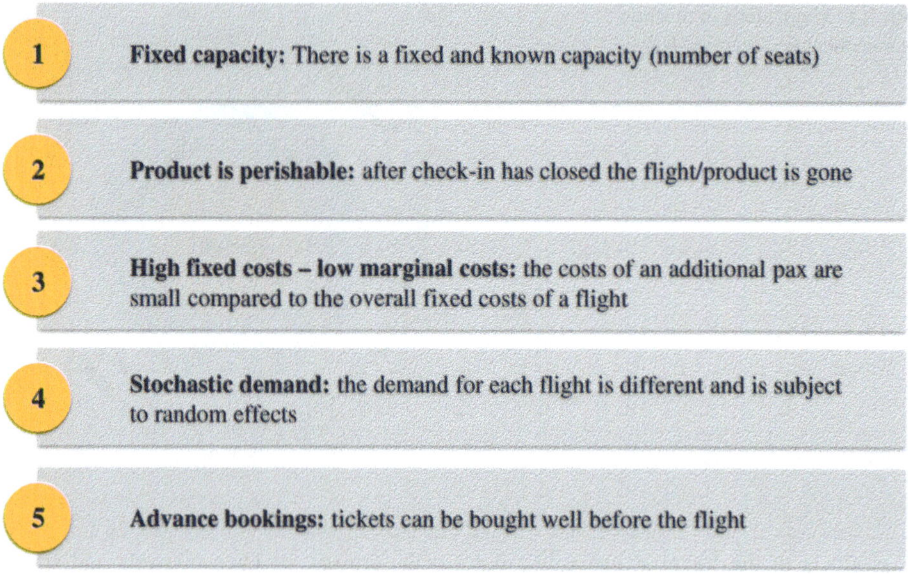

1	**Fixed capacity:** There is a fixed and known capacity (number of seats)
2	**Product is perishable:** after check-in has closed the flight/product is gone
3	**High fixed costs – low marginal costs:** the costs of an additional pax are small compared to the overall fixed costs of a flight
4	**Stochastic demand:** the demand for each flight is different and is subject to random effects
5	**Advance bookings:** tickets can be bought well before the flight

Fig. 1.2 Overview of prerequisites for applying revenue management

1.2 The Rationale for Applying Revenue Management

Throughout this section, we will illustrate in a simplified example the main mechanisms and highlight the relevance and impact of revenue management in practice.

Figure 1.3 shows the seat map of an Airbus A320. The overall capacity of this aircraft amounts to 180 seats in a full economy class configuration. This aircraft is supposed to operate a flight from origin A to destination B on a certain day. The fundamental task of a revenue manager is to fill the 180 seats with the highest possible total revenue. In this example, we ignore the potential impact of ancillary products and services, which have become very relevant in airline distribution in recent years. Instead, we fully focus on the pure and immediate revenue from ticket sales.[2]

The demand for a single flight can come from various customer groups and segments with quite different willingness to pay and product preferences. Knowing the corresponding customer groups and their preferences has become essential in recent years, as we observe a stronger focus on customer centricity in the travel industry. In our example, we assume that four customer segments have a relevant demand for our example flight:

---

[2] In Chap. 6, we will discuss the relevance of ancillary revenues in depth.

1.2 The Rationale for Applying Revenue Management

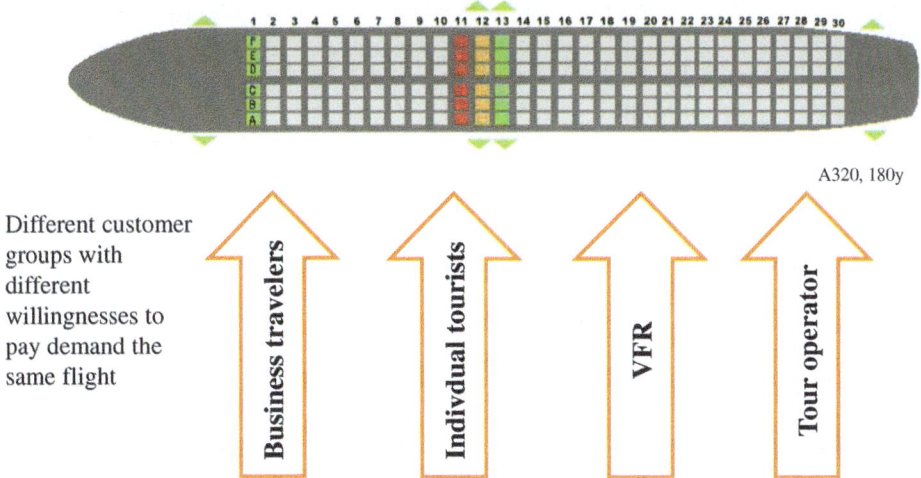

Fig. 1.3 Different customer segments have demand for a limited number of seats on a certain flight

1. **Business travelers** tend to have a short-term booking behavior and a preference for more flexibility, as their plans might change at short notice. On average, they usually have a higher willingness to pay than leisure customers do.
2. **Individual tourists** as a customer group have generally become a lot more important driven by the growth in online travel distribution and the rise of low-cost carriers. While in practice this customer group in total is rather heterogeneous, we assume for the sake of simplicity that a leisure customer traveling individually has a slightly lower willingness to pay than a typical business traveler does.
3. **VFR (Visiting friends and relatives)**: This customer group is also referred to as "ethnic traffic." Nonetheless, the wording "visiting friends and relatives" has become more commonly used. We assume that there is a relevant demand for our flight from this customer group with a rather price-sensitive demand, as they belong to the wider segment of leisure travelers.
4. **Tour operator**: Demand for flight capacities from tour operators can be quite substantial in some markets. We assume that this also holds for our example flight. Nonetheless, tour operators typically seek to get price advantages from contracting a significant volume of seats. Therefore, we assume that the willingness to pay for this customer group is the lowest compared to the other customer segments.

Table 1.1 summarizes the corresponding assumptions for our example flight. Business travelers exhibit the highest willingness to pay with €200 per seat. Overall, there is a demand for 50 seats coming from this customer segment. The customer group of individual tourists has a willingness to pay of €150 per seat with a total demand of 40 seats. Finally, VFR customers exhibit a willingness to pay of €100, while the demand equals 50 seats. Tour operators seek to contract 100 seats at a price of €50. The overall demand for the flight

Table 1.1 Assumed willingness to pay and demand per customer type for hypothetical example flight

Customer type	Demand (unconstrained)	Willingness to pay [€]	Revenue gain [€]	Cumulative demand
Business traveler	50	200	10,000	50
Individual tourists	40	150	6000	90
VFR	50	100	5000	140
Tour operator	100	50	5000	240

from the various customers groups amounts to 240 seats and exceeds the total capacity of 180 seats.

The primary task of the revenue manager is to decide about the optimal capacity allocation, which maximizes the revenue of this flight. In this simple example, the solution is quite easy and obvious. As we need to secure seats for those customers with the highest willingness to pay in order to maximize the revenue, we need to protect 50 seats for the business travelers, 40 seats for individual tourists, 50 seats for VFR customers, and finally, we will give 40 seats to the tour operator, which has the lowest willingness to pay. That means we are constraining the demand for tour operators to just 40 seats, as we protect seats for customers with a higher willingness to pay.[3]

If we now also allow for a time sequence, i.e., the tour operator demand comes first, it implies that we refuse current certain demand in favor of future uncertain demand with a higher willingness to pay. This statement is crucial for the understanding of the idea behind revenue management. Again, in this simplified example, we make a trade-off between current certain demand and future uncertain demand. To put it differently, we are actively refusing current demand with an in average lower willingness to pay in favor of future uncertain demand with an in average higher willingness to pay.

Figure 1.4 translates the unconstrained demand as given in Table 1.1 into a standard demand or price-quantity curve.

1.3 Fundamental KPIs Used in Airline Revenue Management

We imagine that our flight, as described above, operates from Frankfurt to Barcelona (FRA-BCN). The geographical distance of this route amounts to 1265 km. This information is needed to compute some of the core KPIs used in revenue management, which we will present and discuss throughout this section.

---

[3] Of course, in practice the commercial relationship between an airline and a tour operator is often based on a long-term cooperation. Therefore, the capacity allocation might change in reality, when strategic commercial partnership values are taken into consideration.

1.3 Fundamental KPIs Used in Airline Revenue Management

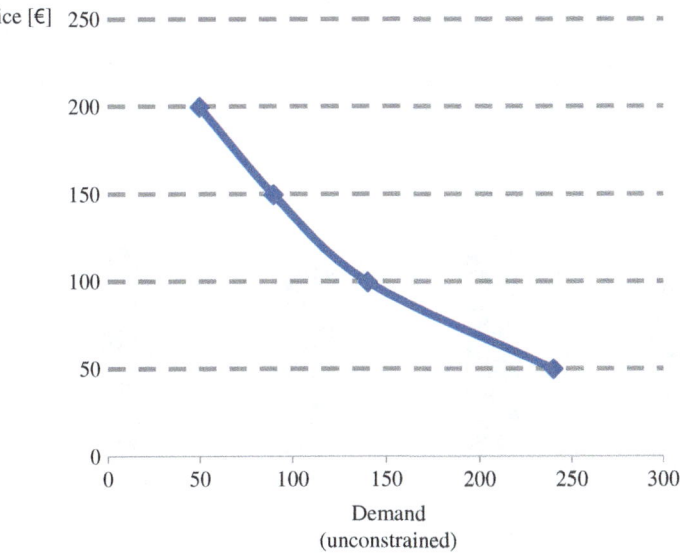

Fig. 1.4 Price-quantity curve for hypothetical example flight

As flights can differ in seat capacities and geographical distances, it is common to use available seat kilometers[4] (ASK) to represent the actual capacity offered in a market. For our example flight the ASK can be easily computed by

$$ASK = \text{distance} \times \text{seat capacity} = 1265\,\text{km} \times 180\,\text{seats} = 227{,}700.$$

As the total revenue of our flight amounts to €23,000, as shown in Table 1.1, we can now calculate the revenue per ASK (RASK). The RASK is one of the most crucial KPIs in airline revenue management.

$$RASK = \text{revenue}/ASK = €23{,}000/227{,}700 = 10.10 \text{ cent}.$$

That means that the airline earns for each seat flown by one kilometer 10.10 cents regardless of the seat being taken or not. RASK is also referred to as unit revenue, as it indicates how much an airline receives for one unit of production, i.e., a seat flown by one kilometer. Similarly, unit costs for airlines are usually described by costs per ASK (CASK).[5] The differential between RASK and CASK determines the profitability of an airline.

---

[4] Instead of kilometers, miles are also frequently used to measure distances in practice. The choice for one or the other is typically determined by the geographical location of a company.

[5] In some cases, it can be useful to regard the CASK excluding fuel costs, as it describes the structural costs of an airline.

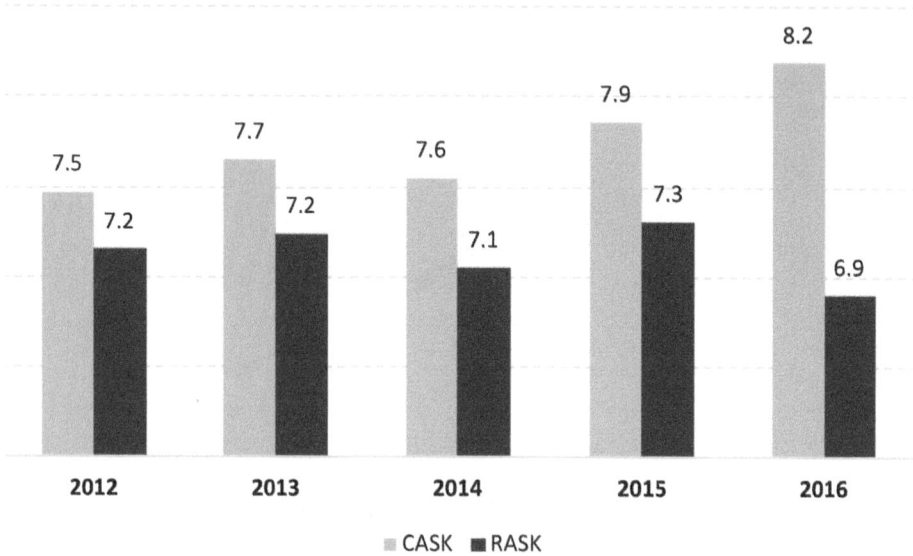

Fig. 1.5 RASK and CASK development, Air Berlin PLC, 2012–2016, in €-cent

To highlight the importance of these two KPIs, Fig. 1.5 shows the RASK and CASK development of Air Berlin during the period 2012 until 2016. While the RASK ranges slightly above 7 € cent on average, the CASK increases to 8.2 € cent and is larger than the RASK in each year, which translated into heavy losses for Air Berlin and finally led to its insolvency in 2017.

1.4 Practitioner View: Balancing Yield and Load Factor

Generally, the aim of a revenue management department will be to maximize revenues, which in turn means to maximize the unit revenues measured through RASK. In practice, demand is subject to random effects and strongly depends on the competitive situation and behavior in a market or on a specific route. At the same time, different combinations of yield per pax and load factor can lead to the same revenue on a flight and finally RASK, e.g., a high load factor and a moderate yield per pax or alternatively a moderate load factor and a high yield per pax can result in the same RASK. This brings us to the question: what is the superior strategy for revenue management, focusing on yield per pax or load factor? Figure 1.6 shows different variables and perspectives, which might affect the optimal balance between the two of them.

Typically, there will be no precise answer to this question. The market position, the product offer, and the overall strategy of the airline will frequently affect the answer. In a market with fierce competition, running a high yield strategy will be basically impossible, as market players will seek to protect their market shares by offering low average prices.

The revenue management strategy will also be determined by the overall strategy of an airline and the underlying business model. In a strict low-cost business model, it will be

1.4 Practitioner View: Balancing Yield and Load Factor

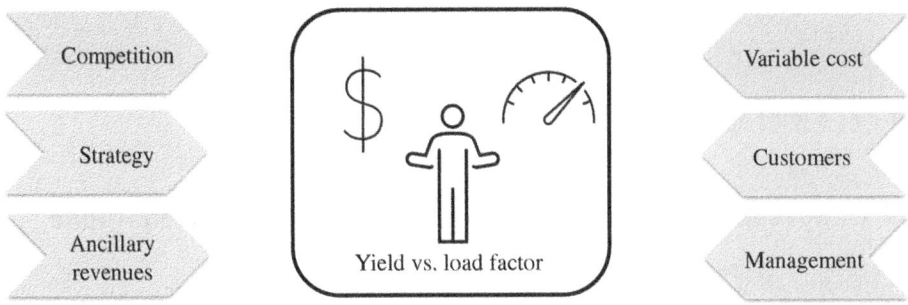

Fig. 1.6 The most important ingredients affecting the overall revenue management strategy

essential to offer attractive prices in the market in order to position the product and the brand accordingly, which might constraint price potentials at the upper end of the pricing grid. Companies like Ryanair have clearly positioned their brand as being price aggressive. Customer perception requires cheap price offers to maintain this brand positioning, while a mathematical revenue optimization might deliver other outcomes.

Furthermore, ancillary revenues have become an integral part of an airline's income since the late 1990s. With each additional passenger on board an aircraft, the airline obtains the opportunity to generate income from sales of additional products and services, such as advance seat reservation, meals, baggage, or inflight entertainment. Airlines with a high share of ancillary revenues compared to their total income will usually focus on a load factor-driven revenue management strategy, as low average ticket prices will be compensated by other revenue sources.[6]

On routes with high variable costs, e.g., arising from airport fees, the possibilities for aggressive prices are naturally limited.

In addition, the customer mix on a route determines the balance between yield per pax and load factor. Typically, routes with a high share of business customers will exhibit a rather short-term booking curve, as business travelers tend to book at a later point in time compared to leisure customers. This short-term business demand is frequently referred to as being yieldable, as business travelers tend to be less price-sensitive than leisure customers. That implies that only to some extent price decreases will stimulate the demand of business travelers. Hence, on routes with strong business demand, it might be reasonable to run a yield-oriented revenue management strategy, as lowering prices might only dilute unit revenues, as the impact on the load factor will be too low to compensate for the loss of yield per passenger.

Finally, management will often interfere with operational revenue management decisions, as there is a direct linkage to the cash flow management of the whole company, which is, of course, a core task of the management board.

---

[6] We will highlight the mechanisms between ticket and ancillary revenues in detail in Chap. 6.

Fig. 1.7 Schematic commercial value chain of an airline

1.5 Revenue Management Within the Value Chain of an Airline

The importance of revenue management for airlines has been constantly growing with unit revenues being constantly under pressure since the early 1990s. This makes revenue management a decisive lever for the overall profitability of an airline. Therefore, revenue management is often the last resort within an airline's organization to optimize and affect the commercial performance from a short-term perspective.

Figure 1.7 gives a simplified high-level overview of the commercial value chain of an airline. While the strategy and capacity planning processes start with a lead-time of many months or years, revenue management is the last unit to affect the short-term development of revenues significantly.

An effective and modern revenue management organization will always be strongly integrated into the wider commercial area and closely interact with sales and marketing teams along the commercial value chain. Otherwise, there will be the risk of lowering prices more than required in periods of weak demand, as sales and marketing on the one hand, and revenue management processes, on the other hand, are not fully aligned and coordinated. This naturally leads to inefficiencies and potentially to substantial losses of revenues. Particularly, in organizations, where sales and marketing and revenue management work mostly independent of each other, the influence on revenue management from the airline's management board will be usually quite high, as it offers an easy but inefficient way to mitigate commercial deficiencies in earlier parts of the commercial value chain. In practice, one of the most frequent mistakes in commercial airline management is to design revenue management as an isolated monolith, which hardly interacts with other commercial units in the organization or barely focuses on the needs of the customers.

Concisely, the role of revenue management is to develop and implement actions to realize market potentials by offering suitable capacity, for the potential customers, at a competitive price at the right point of time.

1.6 Challenge: Seasonality of Demand

We already stressed in the previous section that future demand is stochastic, as it is exposed to random effects. Typically, demand exhibits seasonal patterns or a so-called seasonality.

Generally, in statistics, a time series, e.g., demand for a flight over a certain period, can be decomposed into different components. The idea is that a time series is a composition of components such as trend, random effects, or seasonality.

1.7 Demand Curve Revisited

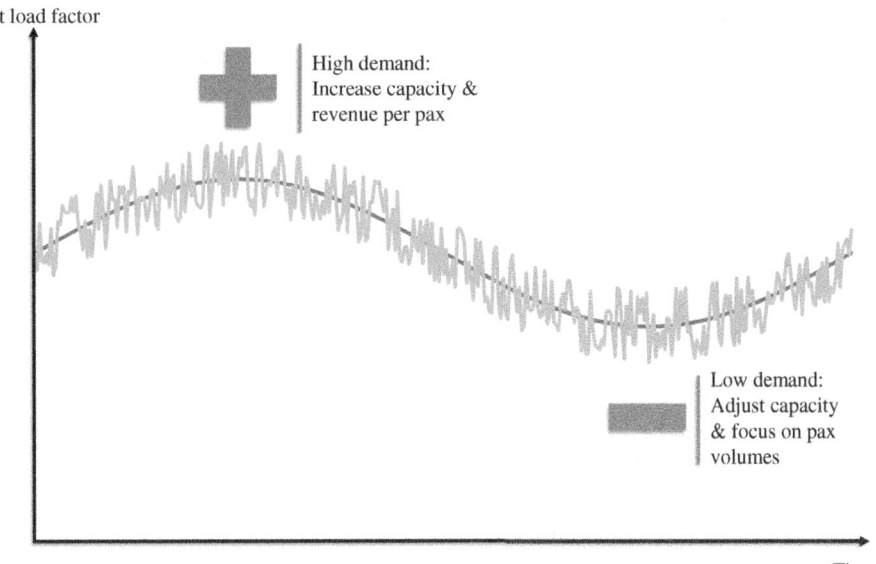

Fig. 1.8 Schematic seasonality pattern of an airline

Figure 1.8 shows, how the seat load factor schematically fluctuates around a seasonal pattern. The task of revenue management is to install high average prices in times of strong demand from the market, while in periods of low demand a focus will be on generating sufficient passenger volumes in order to obtain a sufficient baseload.

1.7 Demand Curve Revisited

The rationale for revenue management is directly related to the classical demand curve, which is part of any elementary course in macroeconomics. The demand curve depicts the relationship between price and quantity. While organizationally a pricing department determines the price grids, revenue management allocates the optimal capacities or quantities to the corresponding price grids, which are typically represented by reservation classes.[7] Figure 1.9 shows the revenue potential associated with an increasing number of price points. In case an airline offers only one rigid price point, the revenue will amount $P_1 Q_1$. With the introduction of two further price points P_2 and P_3, the total revenue will grow to the total of the three gray shaded areas, which is obviously larger than the revenue collected with just one single price point. Revenue management controls and optimizes the availability and capacity for each of these price grids, while pricing defines, designs, and

---

[7] At this point, we will not discuss the fundamentals of pricing in more detail. In practice, each reservation class consists of several fare basis codes, each having separate rules and conditions.

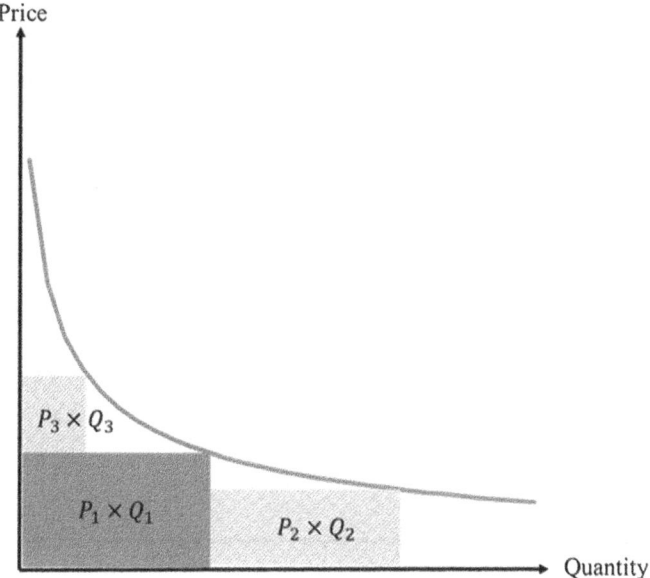

Fig. 1.9 Demand curve with additional price points

conceptualizes them. The target, of course, is to skim the consumer's maximum willingness to pay, which is in terms of economics closely linked to the concept of consumer surplus. That means that the pattern and slope of the demand curve finally determine the optimal capacity allocation by reservation class.

1.8 Checkpoint Chap. 1

This chapter has given a comprehensive overview of the rationales, prerequisites, and principles of revenue management. The key topics from this chapter were:

- Prerequisites for applying revenue management
- Computation and meaning of RASK
- Trade-off between yield per passenger and load factor
- The importance of revenue management in the overall commercial value chain including tasks and responsibilities
- The relevance of seasonality in demand for flights
- Coordinated approaches of revenue and capacity management

1.8 Checkpoint Chap. 1

The reader should now be able to answer the following questions:

1. What are the prerequisites for applying revenue management?
2. An aircraft has 220 seats. 210 passengers have booked the flight with an average yield per passenger of €110. The distance of the flight amounts 1000 km. Compute the corresponding RASK.
3. What is the relevance of seasonality in revenue management? How does it relate to capacity management?
4. How do ancillary revenues basically affect revenue management decisions?

Computerized Revenue Management

2

So far, we have highlighted and discussed on a rather intuitive basis the fundamental mechanisms and ideas of revenue management. In practice, revenue management is done with the help of IT systems. In this chapter, we will outline, how these so-called revenue management systems work in principle. We will go through the major steps of these systems and explain each of them in more detail throughout the next chapters.

2.1 Process Flow of a Revenue Management System

Traditional revenue management systems follow four major steps, as we have already briefly explained at the beginning of Chap. 1. Figure 2.1 shows this typical process flow. In the following, we will go through each of these steps and explain the corresponding backgrounds and concepts in detail.

Revenue management requires data, as it is built on statistical methods and approaches. Therefore, the first step in revenue management will always be **data collection**. Classical revenue management systems rely on data, such as historical passenger volumes, fare basis, compartment, aircraft type including seat capacity, etc. The data will be needed on a single flight event basis, i.e., date, flight number, and departure/arrival time. Furthermore, it will be essential to obtain information about no-shows, cancelations as well as group bookings. Besides the historical time series information, of course, also current data will be required in order to incorporate the most recent booking and demand situation into the revenue

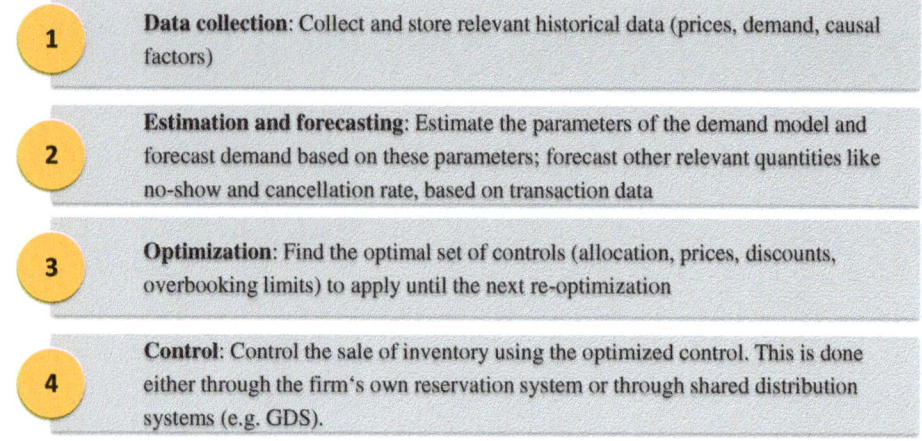

Fig. 2.1 General process flow of a revenue management system

management process. Finally, information about the prices of competitors is usually an additional variable to consider, when it comes to forecasting.[1]

While the data collection process, in general, might appear as an obvious and straightforward step, a rigorous and consistent data quality management within the data collection step will be crucial for forecasting and finally optimization. If the data accuracy is poor, the results of forecasting and optimization will be biased and deliver misleading conclusions, which will worsen the economic performance of the airline, as the price offer in the market will not coincide with actual demand. Setting up the data collection process correctly and efficiently will be focal for both existing and newly implemented revenue management systems.

The data feed into the system runs fully automated and is supported by modern technical interfaces into other operational systems or the company's data warehouse. The revenue management system loads and processes these information from the different data sources in all the subsequent major process steps.

Figure 2.2 provides a schematic overview of a revenue management system incorporating the explanations around the data collection step, as given above. The data collection layer stands at the beginning of the revenue management's process chain.

The core of the revenue management system consists of the actual revenue management model, which involves the estimation or forecasting step, and finally the optimization part, which again depends on the results of the demand forecasts. Particularly in large airline organizations, the revenue management model shows a high degree of automation with little human interference.

---

[1] E-commerce related variables such as look-to-book ratios on the own website or customer profiles can be additional sources of information for revenue management. Particularly in the recent years, the relevance of this data has continuously increased.

2.1 Process Flow of a Revenue Management System

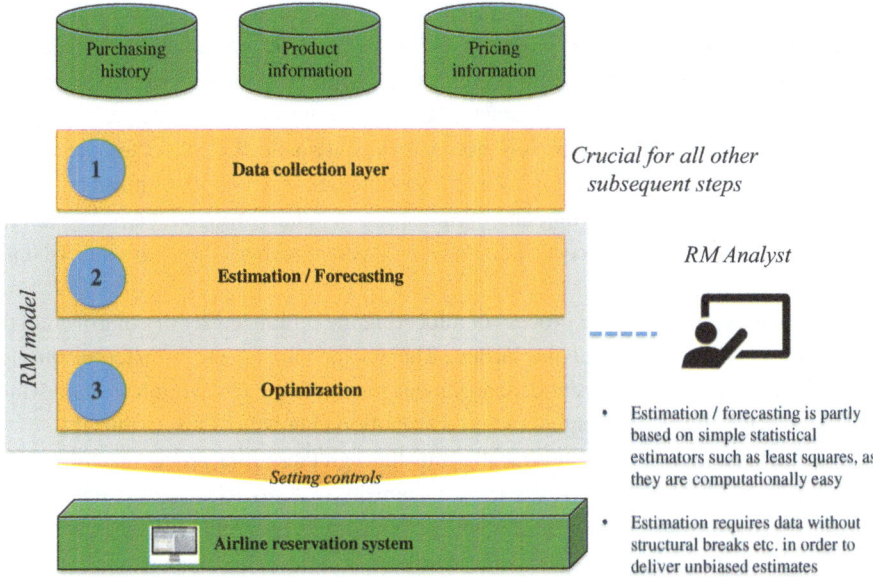

Fig. 2.2 Schematic overview of a revenue management system

However, any automated system has its limitations. A classical revenue management system uses historical data in order to make predictions and finally capacity allocations for future flights. Concisely, a revenue management system makes forecasts about the future based on past data dynamics. While in practice this is often taken for granted, it certainly requires some more explanations to be fully aware of the statistical implications and backgrounds.

Statisticians often use the concept of a so-called data-generating process. The idea of the data-generating process is that there is a true model, which generates the actual data. With the help of statistical methods, we estimate the true values behind the data-generating process. In the simplest case, this data-generating process does not change over time and remains steady. Of course, in reality, it does change quite frequently. Reasons for these changes might be various, e.g., change of competition in a market, crisis events like COVID-19 or 9/11, shift of school holidays, or just a trade fair at a destination, which positively affects demand to a particular destination during a certain period. In these cases, the revenue management analyst needs to adjust the mechanical revenue management model based on the most actual market information and insights. In Fig. 2.2, the dotted line on the right-hand sight from the revenue management analyst to the model depicts this possibility of human interference into this highly automated process.

That means that in these cases the appropriate way to influence the results of the revenue management system will be through changing the parameters and assumptions of the underlying demand model. Fundamental market disruptions like the COVID-19 crisis with a unique impact on customer preferences and travel opportunities in general will require different approaches, which we will partially discuss at a later point in time throughout this book, particularly in Chap. 7.

The **forecasting** step uses the historical data to estimate the underlying parameters of the demand model. This allows us to derive conclusions about the total market demand including price elasticities. Besides the demand parameters, other variables such as no-shows and cancelations will be estimated throughout the forecasting step.

Finally, the **optimization** step uses the estimated demand and allocates the aircraft capacity in such a way that the total expected revenue on a flight is maximized.

We will address both forecasting and optimization in detail throughout Chaps. 3 and 4, where we will also present the corresponding statistical concepts as well as some first use cases.

The **control** step refers to the process of allocating the optimized set of controls into the sales and distribution system of the airline. The set of controls are transferred through technical interfaces from the revenue management system to the reservation system, which itself is connected to the different sales and distribution channels of the airline.

A revenue management system typically runs through these four process steps continuously, e.g., once a day. Some revenue management systems even allow for intraday optimization. With each of these cycles, the system stores and archives the most recent booking data, generating a so-called data collection point. This data is then used for re-forecasting and re-optimization.

2.2 Limitations of Fully Automated Revenue Management

So far, we have introduced and discussed the general processes and system approach for fully automated revenue management, as frequently used in large network carrier environments. The process flow as described before might awaken the impression that revenue management is always fully automated. In this section, we want to describe and explain situations, in which fully automated revenue management is not possible. At the same time, we will present some simple and intuitive alternatives.

Already in the previous section, we have discussed some practical challenges around the data collection process. These challenges might be so significant in some cases that fully automated revenue management is not possible delivering biased and misleading results. In the following, we will further elaborate on the most relevant cases, in which automated revenue management will not be effective, while other approaches might be more promising.

Whenever the historical data used for the forecast and the estimation of the demand model is missing or becomes unreliable, automated revenue management will have certain limitations. Changes in the underlying market environment may have different causes such as:

- Competitive landscape, e.g., a new competitor enters/leaves a route or increases/decreases capacity
- Overall demand, e.g., as a result of an economic crisis
- Seasonality, e.g., shift of school holidays from one year to another

2.2 Limitations of Fully Automated Revenue Management

- Data errors, e.g., as a result of technical problems in the data collection layer

Furthermore, capacity might be unstable, e.g., due to a change of aircraft equipment for operational reasons, violating the prerequisites for applying revenue management, as shown in Chap. 1, Sect. 1.1. Blocked seats or tour operator allotments may also be reasons for a change of capacity during the sales period affecting the precision of the forecast. Whenever an airline enters a new route with unknown demand patterns, sufficient and reliable historical demand data will be crucial for applying automated revenue management techniques. Finally, a significant change of an airline's marketing strategy, e.g., aggressive price campaigns in the past, might affect the estimated demand model, as predicted by the revenue management system.

Rule-based revenue management can offer an intuitive way to overcome these data deficiencies and violations of prerequisites. The idea of rule-based revenue management is to define and set rules within the system, which constrain the capacity by reservation class. Usually, these rules rely on core variables such as load factor or simply days before departure. Figure 2.3 shows two examples of such simple rules. On the left-hand side we see, how capacity steering could look like in case the load factor is the trigger for opening or closing a certain booking class (Y, M, T, L have been arbitrarily chosen). In this example, reservation class L would close after the flight has reached a load factor of 30%. Assuming a capacity of 180 seats, it means that after 54 passengers have booked this flight, the L class will no longer be available. Similarly, class T closes after the flight is booked by 50% corresponding to 90 passengers. Finally, the Y class remains open during the entire sales period until the flight is fully booked. The intuition behind this rule is quite easy: as demand grows for our flight, less valuable booking classes will be closed in order to protect seats for customers with a higher willingness to pay.

On the right-hand side of Fig. 2.3, the example shows a slightly more sophisticated rule. Based on this rule the four reservation classes open and close in a combination of certain days before departure and booking levels. The numbers in the gray shaded fields correspond to AUs.[2] The example reads as follows: Between 80 and 100 days before the departure, booking class L is open for up to 50 passengers. Regardless of the booking level, the L class will close at latest 80 days before departure. Hence, even if the flight is completely empty, the L class will have no availability. The T class has an AU of 100 seats for up to 60 days before departure. That means the T class would be sold out, if

- 100 passengers have booked the flight in the sales period greater than 60 days before departure or
- The remaining sales period is smaller than 60 days regardless of the booking count.

---

[2] AU stands for authorized capacity. An AU of 180 means that 180 seats are available in a certain booking class. AU is a frequently used terminology in revenue management systems.

Load factor	Y	M	T	L
10%	OPEN	OPEN	OPEN	OPEN
20%	OPEN	OPEN	OPEN	OPEN
30%	OPEN	OPEN	OPEN	OPEN
40%	OPEN	OPEN	OPEN	CLOSED
50%	OPEN	OPEN	OPEN	CLOSED
60%	OPEN	OPEN	CLOSED	CLOSED
70%	OPEN	OPEN	CLOSED	CLOSED
80%	OPEN	OPEN	CLOSED	CLOSED
90%	OPEN	CLOSED	CLOSED	CLOSED
100%	OPEN	CLOSED	CLOSED	CLOSED

Days before departure	Y	M	T	L
100	180	150	100	50
90	180	150	100	50
80	180	150	100	50
70	180	150	100	0
60	180	150	100	0
50	180	150	0	0
40	180	150	0	0
30	180	150	0	0
20	180	0	0	0
10	180	0	0	0

Fig. 2.3 Example for simple rule-based revenue management

The motivation for a rule including days before departure could be that certain customer segments exhibit price-inelastic demand. Let us think of a business traveler, who needs to get on a certain flight due to an important meeting on a specific day. His decision for or against this flight is mainly determined by the obligation to attend the meeting at the planned time, while the price plays a less decisive role. Therefore, on routes with strong demand from business travelers, a rule based on days before departure might be useful to capture the customers' maximum willingness to pay.

Of course, the rules, as described here in this section, have limitations of their own. In practice, these rules can be augmented by extensive data analysis incorporating different views and angles including an expert assessment of a revenue management analyst, which can be precious and effective particularly in times of rapid market changes.

2.3 Checkpoint Chap. 2

In this chapter, we have discussed the key concepts and approaches of computerized revenue management. We went through the main steps of a revenue management system and addressed the limitations of fully automated revenue management systems. The key topics from this chapter were:

- Process flow of revenue management systems
- Limitations of automated revenue management
- Rule-based revenue management

The reader should now be able to answer the following questions:

1. State and explain the general steps in computerized revenue management.
2. What is the idea of rule-based revenue management?
3. Please give reasons including a short explanation, why automated revenue management might deliver biased results. How do crisis events like the COVID-19 pandemic potentially affect your results?

Estimation and Forecasting 3

In the previous chapters, we have laid the foundations of revenue management. We have shown and explained that a revenue management system requires estimation and forecasting techniques in order to make predictions about quantities like demand, price elasticity, no-show rate, etc. The quality and the precision of the estimates and forecasts are crucial, as they directly affect the optimization results and finally the overall revenue generated. Hence, the quality of forecasting and estimations influences the bottom-line performance and finally the profitability of an airline.[1]

At the same time, it is important to understand that a forecast is not a single number or just a point estimate. A forecast needs to be understood in statistical terms exhibiting a forecast error and a prediction interval. That means that the forecast itself is a random variable. Hence, the single-point estimate, which managers often tend to focus on in practice, will rarely be accurate.

In the following, we will first explain the practical relevance with some actual example data. We will then introduce some of the most frequently used forecasting methods in revenue management based on classical time-series statistics. In the last chapter of this book, we will present how data science can help to improve forecasting and revenue management as such.

3.1 Practical Relevance of Estimation and Forecasting

The daily work routine of a revenue manager involves the frequent analysis and assessment of data beyond the widely automated process of a modern revenue management system.

---

[1] Poelt (1998) argues that a 20% reduction of forecast error translates into a 1% incremental revenue increase.

Figure 3.1 shows a typical booking curve for a single flight, which a revenue management system might display to a revenue manager. The booking curve or booking profile exhibits, how bookings develop toward the day of departure. Let us assume that 365 days before departure a flight opens for sales. The booking curve describes how bookings grow during this period until departure. In Fig. 3.1, the gray line represents the booking curve for the current year, the black one for the previous year. The curve for the previous year is supposed to be a reference for the development of the current year. That requires that the two flights are comparable in terms of demand patterns. In the last year, the flight departed with a load factor of about 80%, as the black line indicates. Currently, the flight has a load factor of roughly 40%, which is substantially above the level of last year at the same point measured against time until departure. The load factor is approximately 20 percentage points higher in comparison to the year before, while the slope of this year's booking curve is much steeper.

The task of revenue management is now to make an assessment and analysis about the most likely future development of bookings. In statistical terms, revenue management is required to make a forecast based on an estimated demand model.

Figure 3.1 shows in a very intuitive way, why an accurate forecast is so essential. If we overestimate future demand, we will lose revenues, as seats will remain empty, which could have been filled otherwise. If we underestimate future demand, we will again lose revenues, as we could have sold the seats at a higher yield per passenger by protecting seats for customers with a higher willingness to pay. Only in the case of an unbiased demand or booking forecast, the revenue management process will deliver an optimal capacity allocation reflecting the actual demand situation and leading to a maximization of revenues.

A first naïve forecast for the flight depicted in Fig. 3.1, based on an extrapolation of the current positive deviation against the previous year and assuming last year's slope of the booking curve, would yield that the flight is likely to be fully booked reaching a load factor of about 100%.

A pure analysis of the time series as such to derive a statistical prediction about the future is also referred to as a dynamic forecast. Dynamic emphasizes the focus on the pure dynamics of the time series itself without incorporating the impact of other variables, e.g., such as own or competitive prices.

In Fig. 3.2, the demand on a certain route is presented from a different perspective. The graph shows the cumulative demand per booking class for a route in the German domestic market[2] for all flights in one month. Booking class A has the lowest value in terms of average willingness to pay and unit revenue, while booking class J ranks highest.

Opposite to the dynamic view described above, Fig. 3.2 shows the development of demand dependent on the booking classes, i.e., price levels capturing customers' different

---

[2] The naming of the booking classes has been arbitrarily changed to A–J in order to anonymize the data, which has been sourced from a major German airline for pure scientific purposes.

3.1 Practical Relevance of Estimation and Forecasting 23

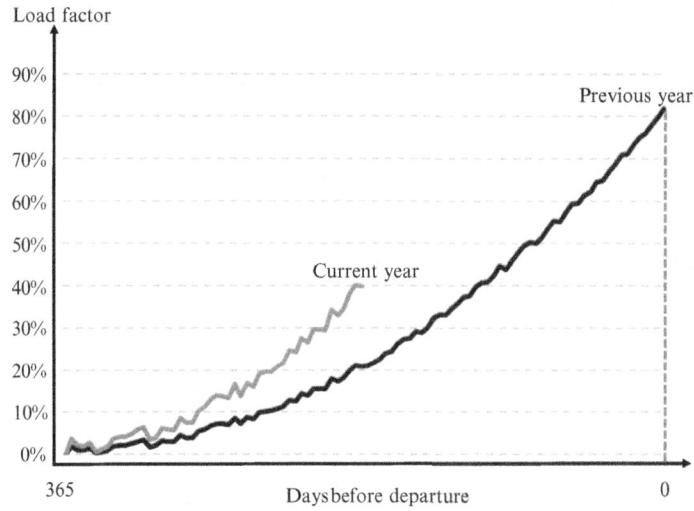

Fig. 3.1 Booking curve for a single flight event, current year versus previous year

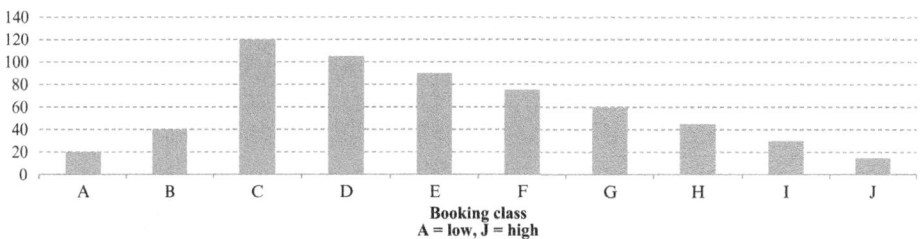

Fig. 3.2 Cumulative observed demand per booking class on a single route

willingness to pay. Therefore, this view is referred to as a static view, which is the basis for a static forecast.

The demand per booking class, as given in Fig. 3.2, clearly shows the impact of revenue management on realized bookings on this route. As the booking classes A–J are proxies for the price intervals, we could expect from an economic perspective that with higher booking classes, demand will decrease. This expected pattern is observable for classes C–J, while for A and B the opposite is true contradicting economic intuition. This is a direct result and consequence of revenue management.

As explained before, revenue management aims at maximizing the revenue on a flight by protecting seats for customers with the highest willingness to pay. If the lowest booking classes A and B would be open and available for the entire sales period of the flight, the aircraft would be filled with a high fraction of customers with a low willingness to pay leading to a suboptimal revenue result for this flight. In order to maximize revenues, it is the task of revenue management to constrain the capacity allocation of the lowest booking classes to protect capacities for demand with a higher willingness to pay. The fact that the lowest booking classes A and B exhibit a lower cumulative booking count than the next higher-class C is evidence for revenue management constraining the capacity in reservation classes attracting demand of customers with a low willingness to pay. In a revenue management system or a data warehouse, the booking data observed and stored only represents constrained demand, which is a challenge, when it comes to optimization, as the data might suggest that demand grows, as prices increase, which would obviously lead to misleading results in terms of capacity allocations. In order to come to a view on real and true demand, unconstraining observed demand is a crucial step in revenue management. A systematic unconstraining of demand data has to be done before the actual forecast can be calculated.

Similar to the explanations given above, it will be essential that forecasting delivers an unbiased result for future expected demand, as otherwise, the revenue management process in total will deliver nonoptimal capacity allocations with potentially negative impacts on profitability. Finally, the unconstraining step itself is an estimate of true demand based on observed booking counts.

Figure 3.3 is an augmented version of Fig. 10.2 incorporating the unconstraining of demand taking place prior to the actual forecasting step.

So far, we have highlighted the fundamental differences between dynamic and static forecasts. Of course, one can also think of mixed forecasts using both static and dynamic forecasts at the same time in order to reduce the resulting forecast error.

In classical revenue management systems, the forecasting algorithms are not particularly complicated, as within a rather short period of time, e.g., in a nightly batch process, as described in Fig. 3.3, a substantial amount of parameters and variables have to be forecasted. Therefore, there will be also a need for speed, simplicity, and robustness.

In Chap. 7, we will present and discuss in detail forecasting methods based on data science approaches, which have substantially gained relevance in recent years with growing computational system capabilities and a wider access to data sources. However, the current chapter focuses on classical forecasting methods based on time series analysis and linear regression.

3.2 Unconstraining of Demand Data: EM Algorithm

Following the process flow as given in Fig. 3.3, we will now look at forecasting data, which is only partially observable, as described above and shown in Fig. 3.2.

For correcting constrained data, the expectation–maximization (EM) method is the most frequently used method in revenue management systems. We will now go through the mathematical details of the algorithms, which might be helpful for some readers to understand the capabilities and constraints of the EM algorithm in revenue management systems. For some readers with a strong practical view, this section might only be interesting background information.

3.2 Unconstraining of Demand Data: EM Algorithm

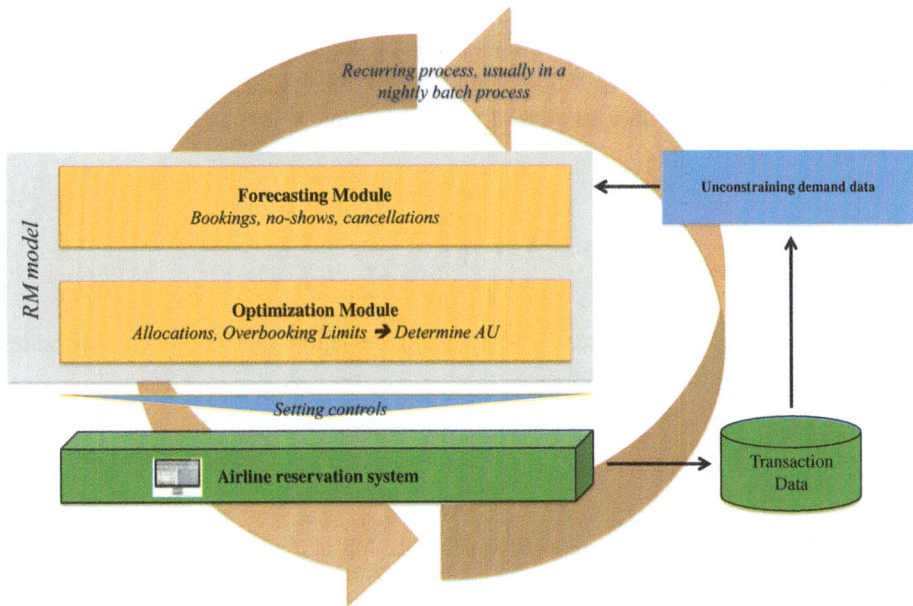

Fig. 3.3 Schematic process flow of a revenue management system including unconstraining of demand data

Let us first outline the assumptions. The first assumption is that demand across products or reservations classes is independent of each other, which might not always be fulfilled in practice, particularly in low-cost carrier environments, where the product specification mostly differs by price exhibiting a significant cross-correlation. Let us suppose that we have $M + N$ observations bookings for a product. These observed bookings are denoted by $y_1, \ldots, y_{M+N}$. The observations do not follow a time series ordering, as they are unsorted generated from a random process.[3] That implies also that seasonality effects or trends, as outlined in Chap. 1, Sect. 1.6, are neglected for the sake of simplicity.[4] M observations are constrained, as the product has not been available anymore, while N observations are constrained. That means that the N observations in Y, which is the corresponding vector of all elements $y_1, \ldots, y_{M+N}$, reflect true demand, while M elements in Y represent observed demand. In order to receive unbiased forecasts, we need to estimate the entire true distribution of Y in order to decide about the optimal capacity allocation.

---

[3] The corresponding random variable is assumed to be i.i.d., which stands for independently and identically distributed. The i.i.d. concept is a well-known terminology in statistics, which we will not discuss in more detail at this point.

[4] The application of the EM algorithm incorporating time series effects will be substantially more complicated and would go beyond the scope of this introductory book, cf. McGill (1995).

Let us further suppose that all observations are generated from a common distribution with observations being randomly constrained by M booking limits $b_1, \ldots, b_M$, which results in $y_1 = b_1, \ldots, y_M = b_M$. N observations are unconstrained.

If all values in Y were unconstrained, the corresponding Gaussian likelihood function would be represented by

$$L(\mu, \sigma, M+N) = \prod_{i=1}^{M+N} \frac{1}{\sigma\sqrt{2\pi}} e^{-\frac{1}{2}\left(\frac{y_i - \mu}{\sigma}\right)^2},$$

with μ and σ denoting the mean and standard deviation of Y. The corresponding log-likelihood function is given by

$$\ln L(\mu, \sigma, M+N) = -\frac{M+N}{2} \ln 2\pi - (M+N) \ln \sigma - \frac{\sum_{i=1}^{M+N}(y_i - \mu)^2}{2\sigma^2}.$$

Finally, the estimators for μ and σ maximizing the log-likelihood function are given by

$$\widehat{\mu} = \frac{1}{M+N} \sum_{i=1}^{M+N} y_i,$$

$$\widehat{\sigma}^2 = \frac{1}{M+N-1} \sum_{i=1}^{M+N} (y_i - \widehat{\mu})^2.$$

As outlined in the assumptions, we actually do not know the true values of the M constrained observations in Y. Therefore, the immediate estimate of the likelihood function is not possible. For this reason, the EM algorithm uses two consecutive steps in order to generate an unbiased estimate for the entire likelihood function:

1. E-step: This step replaces the M censored observations by estimates of their uncensored values using the current estimates of mean and variance.
2. M-step: In this step, the entire log-likelihood function is maximized based on the updated data from the E-step to estimate new values for mean and variance.

These two steps are iteratively repeated until the parameter estimates converge. At this point, we will skip further mathematical details, which the interested reader may find in Talluri and Ryzin (2005) together with other methods of unconstraining.

3.2 Unconstraining of Demand Data: EM Algorithm

In the following, we will illustrate the intuition of the EM algorithm using a simple R code.[5] For this purpose, we generate a normally distributed random variable with a mean of 10 and standard deviation of 1. This random variable Y has 20 true values.

```
> set.seed(123) ## ensures we all see the same output
>
> trueMean <-10 ## suppose this true mean is unknown
>
> n <-20
> y <-rnorm(n, mean = trueMean) ## sample demand data from a normal
distribution
> print(y) ## gives the single values
 [1]  9.439524  9.769823 11.558708 10.070508 10.129288 11.715065
10.460916
 [8]  8.734939 9.313147 9.554338 11.224082 10.359814 10.400771 10.110683
[15]  9.444159 11.786913 10.497850 8.033383 10.701356 9.527209
>
> hist(y, col = "lavender") ## plots the histogram of y
> abline(v = mean(y), col = "red", lwd = 2) ## highlight sample mean
>
> yobs<-y ## observed demand
> yobs[19]<-5 ## demand data is constrained and value set to 5
> yobs[20]<-5 ## demand data is constrained and value set to 5
>
> mean(y) ## returns the mean of true y
[1] 10.14162
> mean(yobs) ## returns the mean of observed y
[1] 9.630196
```

Figure 3.4 shows the histogram for Y. The vertical line exhibits the mean of the 20 true values in Y.

Additionally, we introduce a second variable Y_{obs}, which contains the observed, i.e., constrained, values of Y. In the R code given above, we substitute the true values of $y_{obs,19}$ and $y_{obs,20}$ by a rigid 5, which could be an example of constrained demand. The means of Y and Y_{obs} amount to 10.14 and 9.63, respectively.

In reality, we would not know Y and only observe Y_{obs}, as we do not know the true data-generating process and any immediate linear regression for mean and standard deviation of

---

[5]R is a language and environment for statistical computing and graphics. The code used here can be directly copied into R so that the reader can easily replicate the results as shown here. Parts of the codes have been taken from rpubs.com.

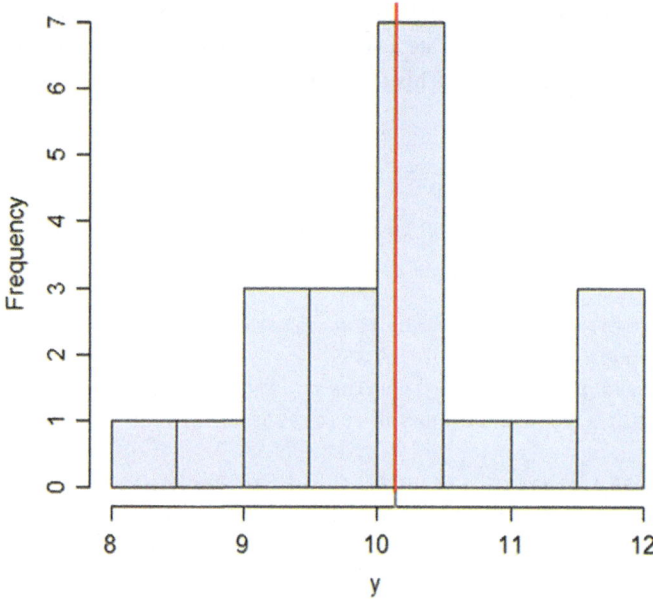

Fig. 3.4 Histogram for true Y as generated from R code

the underlying distribution would be biased, as observations in Y_{obs} are censored as a result of constraining demand in certain booking classes.

With the help of our *R* code, we first assess the likelihood for a certain normal distribution with standard deviation being set to 1 and mean gradually increasing from 1 to 13 in steps of 1. The results are given below.

```
> ## Next: check and compute likelihood of different mean assumptions
step-wise
>
> prod( dnorm( yobs, mean=1, sd=1 ) )
[1] 0
> prod( dnorm( yobs, mean=2, sd=1 ) )
[1] 1.185591e-275
> prod( dnorm( yobs, mean=3, sd=1 ) )
[1] 1.013974e-213
> prod( dnorm( yobs, mean=4, sd=1 ) )
[1] 1.787429e-160
> prod( dnorm( yobs, mean=5, sd=1 ) )
[1] 6.494437e-116
> prod( dnorm( yobs, mean=6, sd=1 ) )
```

(continued)

3.2 Unconstraining of Demand Data: EM Algorithm

```
[1] 4.863674e-80
> prod( dnorm( yobs, mean=7, sd=1 ) )
[1] 7.507543e-53
> prod( dnorm( yobs, mean=8, sd=1 ) )
[1] 2.388589e-34
> prod( dnorm( yobs, mean=9, sd=1 ) )
[1] 1.566374e-24
> prod( dnorm( yobs, mean=10, sd=1 ) )
[1] 2.117191e-23
> prod( dnorm( yobs, mean=11, sd=1 ) )
[1] 5.898408e-31
> prod( dnorm( yobs, mean=12, sd=1 ) )
[1] 3.387037e-47
> prod( dnorm( yobs, mean=13, sd=1 ) )
[1] 4.00881e-72
```

For every mean, we calculate the likelihood function as the product of the individual probabilities for every $y_{obs,i}$. The results of the code suggest that the likelihood function delivers the largest value at a mean of 10. Alternatively, we can produce results that are more reliable by introducing a simple loop, which runs through the interval 7 to 13 in steps of 0.1 through all possible means similar to the manual approach given above.

```
> mean_grid <-seq(7, 13, by=0.1)  ## values of the mean to check the
likelihood at
> myLikelihood <-rep(0, length(mean_grid) )
> for( i in seq_along( myLikelihood ) ) {
+ myLikelihood[i] <-prod( dnorm( xobs, mean = mean_grid[i], sd=1 ) )
+ }
> plot( myLikelihood ~ mean_grid, type="b" )
```

The corresponding result is shown in Fig. 3.5. We can clearly see that the likelihood function reaches its maximum at a value close to 10.

By replacing the censored values in Y_{obs} and estimating a new likelihood function, we could run through several iterations until the mean, at which the likelihood function reaches its maximum, converges. This basically illustrates, how E- and M-step of the EM algorithm work, when applied to an artificial dataset.

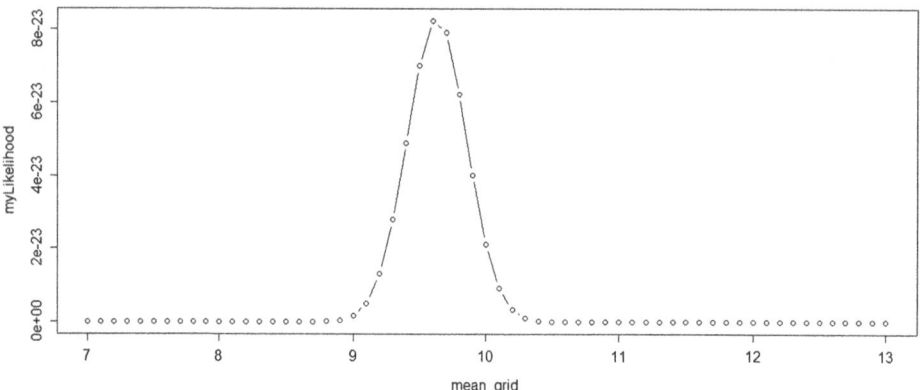

Fig. 3.5 Likelihood function for Y_{obs} dependent on the underlying mean of the normal distribution

Finally, the EM algorithm can also be used to estimate mixtures of multiple distributions, e.g., demand for different booking classes, which is an extension of the univariate one-dimensional problem, as outline here.[6]

Beyond the mathematical and statistical details of the EM algorithm, it is essential to understand that the unconstraining step is essential to generate meaningful forecasting results, as biased results of the unconstraining step will yield biased results in all further steps of the revenue management process.

In the following, we will concentrate on demand forecasting in general. We will focus on simple time-series-based forecasting approaches assuming that the underlying data is unconstrained.

3.3 Pick-up Forecasting

Pick-up forecasting is a simple forecasting method frequently used in revenue management, which exploits the booking pattern of past flights in order to estimate future booking development. That means that pick-up forecasting uses the time series of booking intake and predicts the expected incremental future bookings. In the following, we will use a numerical example to present the method in more detail.

For this purpose, we use artificially produced data for a series of flights departing in the period of 10 June and 17 June 2021, once per day. Further, we look at the incremental bookings for these flights during the last 8 days before departure. Table 3.1 shows the corresponding data and illustrates, how pick-up forecasting generally works.

---

[6]The Mixtools package within *R* offers various possibilities to use the EM algorithm for the case of mixed distributions, cf. https://cran.r-project.org/web/packages/mixtools/mixtools.pdf.

3.3 Pick-up Forecasting

Table 3.1 Applying pick-up forecasting to an artificial example dataset

\multicolumn{9}{l	}{Days before departure}	Departure
8	7	6	5	4	3	2	1	0	date
Incremental bookings									
6	3	11	4	9	8	13	3	13	10.06.2021
8	6	6	3	16	11	5	4	2	11.06.2021
1	2	0	0	3	6	2	6	8	12.06.2021
6	0	4	1	2	6	3	2		13.06.2021
3	8	8	6	5	1	2			14.06.2021
1	0	2	7	6	4				15.06.2021
0	1	1	6	5					16.06.2021
1	11	12	6						17.06.2021
3.3	3.9	5.5	4.1	6.6	6	5	3.8	7.7	Average
Cumulative bookings									
6	9	20	24	33	41	54	57	70	10.06.2021
8	14	20	23	39	50	55	59	61	11.06.2021
1	3	3	3	6	12	14	20	28	12.06.2021
6	6	10	11	13	19	22	24	24 + 7.7	13.06.2021
3	11	19	25	30	31	33	33 + 3.8	36.8 + 7.7	14.06.2021
1	1	3	10	16	20				15.06.2021
0	1	2	8	13					16.06.2021
1	12	24	30						17.06.2021

The upper part of Table 3.1 describes the incremental bookings per flight and day, e.g., six additional passengers booked the flight on 10 June, 8 days prior to departure. Another three passengers booked the same flight 7 days prior to departure and finally, 13 passengers booked on the day of departure. The lower part of Table 3.1 sums up the incremental booking intake per day and flight and shows the corresponding cumulative booking view. Hence, the flights between 10 and 12 June depart with 70, 61, and 28 passengers. The flight on the 13 June has not departed, yet, which implies that today is the 12 June. The task is now to predict the final booking count for the future flights between 13 and 17 June.

The pick-up forecasting method in the additive version makes use of the average historical intake of all flights in the reference group.[7] In the upper part of Table 3.1, we have computed the mean intake for each advance-booking day. The average intake for a flight 8 days prior to departure amounts 3.3 and 7 days prior to departure 3.9 etc. With this information, we can now forecast the expected cumulative booking count for the flight on 13 June, which is simply given by the last observed booking count of 24 plus the average

---

[7] Reference group means that we require a set of comparable or homogenous flights in terms of demand patterns and charcteristics to generate reliable and accurate results. In practice, the creation of an appropriate reference group requires insights about the market or route in scope.

intake on the day of departure, which amounts 7.7. That results in an expected booking count for the flight departing on 13 June of 31.7 passengers, which rounds up to 32 passengers.

In the gray shaded cells in Table 3.1, we have illustrated how the forecast for the two flights departing on 13 and 14 June works. In the same way, we could predict also the booking counts for the other flights shown.

Opposite to the additive pick-up method shown here, the multiplicative pick-up method uses the percentage intake compared to cumulative bookings made.

3.4 Stationary and Nonstationary Time-Series Models

A time series can be stationary or nonstationary, which again has an impact on the forecasting approach and the estimation of the demand model as such. A stationary time series has to fulfill the three following criteria:

1. The mean of the corresponding time series needs to be constant and unchanged over time. In mathematical terms, this mean that $E[y_i] = \mu$ for all $i = 1, \ldots, T$, where E denotes the expected value and T the overall number of random variables.
2. The time series has a finite variance, which can be expressed as $\text{Var}[y_i] < \infty$. If the variance were infinite, it would be violating criterion (1), as the time series would not have a well-defined mean.
3. The autocorrelation and autocovariance of the time series is independent of time shifts, i.e. $\text{Cov}(y_i, y_j) = \text{Cov}(y_{i+s}, y_{j+s})$, where $i \neq j$ and s denotes any arbitrary time shift of the time series.

If one of the three criteria is violated, the time series is classified as nonstationary requiring a different forecasting and estimation approach. Intuitively, any time series with a trend, e.g. a booking pattern, as presented in Fig. 3.1, will typically be nonstationary, which requires some caution, when it comes to inference about the demand model and the expected future bookings.

The autocorrelation functions of both a stationary and nonstationary time series exhibit typical patterns, which we will not discuss at this point, as it would go beyond the scope of this book. A detailed discussion about the characteristics of the autocorrelation functions of stationary and nonstationary variables in the context of revenue management can be found in Talluri and Ryzin (2005). In the following, we will focus on forecasting of stationary variables.

3.5 ARMA Processes

Throughout this section, we will introduce the concept of ARMA processes. ARMA stands for *auto*regressive *m*oving *a*verage. ARMA processes are a frequently used method to model time series in statistics in general and in revenue management in particular. ARMA processes are based on the idea that a current value of a time series can be explained through its past values. That means that a value today consists of a weighted average of past historical values.[8]

Let us start with the simplest case of an autoregressive process of order 1, an AR (1) process, which links a value of the random variable y at time t to its past value y_{t-1}. Mathematically, we can formulate this relationship as follows

$$y_t = \alpha y_{t-1} + u_t,$$

where α denotes a coefficient between -1 and 1, while u_t is an i.i.d. error term with mean 0 and constant variance σ^2. If $|\alpha| > 1$ the time series would become nonstationary, which we will not discuss in more detail.

Figure 3.6 shows the reaction of y to a single random effect of size 1 for different values of α. With α being closer to 1, the effect of this single shock becomes more persistent, while with α being close to 0 the impact of the shock quickly vanishes. That means that α fundamentally determines the dynamics of the time series y. In the following, we will transform this AR(1) process into a moving average representation. For this purpose, we need to understand that the relationship formulated by the AR(1) process holds for any point in time, i.e. t, $t-1$, $t-2$, etc. Therefore, we can rewrite the given AR(1) process for time $t-1$ as follows:

$$y_{t-1} = \alpha y_{t-2} + u_{t-1}.$$

We can now use this equation to substitute for y_{t-1} in the AR(1) process for time t. This yields the following result

$$y_t = \alpha(\alpha y_{t-2} + u_{t-1}) + u_t,$$

which can be rewritten as

---

[8]This requires the data to be free of any structural breaks etc. A change in the underlying market dynamics caused through a major crisis like the COVID-19 pandemic, makes the usage of ARMA modelling difficult and potentially impossible.

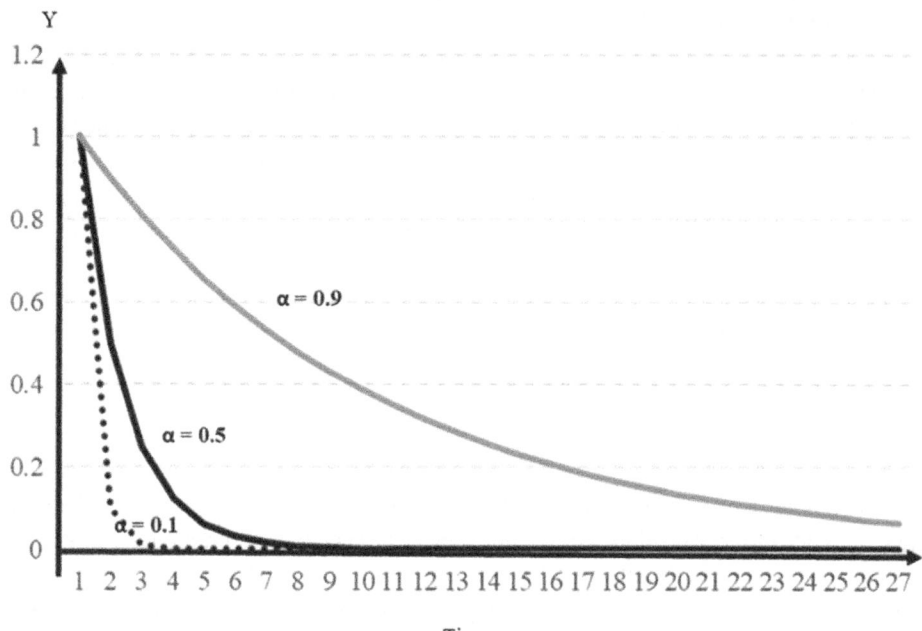

Fig. 3.6 Behavior of an AR(1) process for different values of α

$$y_t = \alpha^2 y_{t-2} + \alpha u_{t-1} + u_t.$$

In a next step, we can again replace y_{t-2} by the corresponding AR(1) relationship, which yields

$$y_t = \alpha^2 (\alpha y_{t-3} + u_{t-2}) + \alpha u_{t-1} + u_t,$$

which finally delivers

$$y_t = \alpha^3 y_{t-3} + \alpha^2 u_{t-1} + \alpha u_{t-1} + u_t.$$

By repeating this process infinitively often, we obtain a representation of y_t solely consisting of past values of the error term u. As we focus on stationary time series, i.e., $|\alpha| < 1$, the term $\alpha^k y_{t-k}$ converges to zero, as k goes toward infinity. Hence, we can finally obtain the following MA representation of our AR(1) process

$$y_t = \sum_{k=0}^{\infty} \alpha^k u_{t-k}.$$

Hence, the time series y can be described either by a weighted average of its own past values or by a weighted average of the underlying error terms, which the time series y was exposed to over time.

ARMA processes offer a very simple but powerful way to model time series variables.

In practice, the M-period moving average forecast and exponential smoothing approach make use of ARMA time series modeling to generate predictions for key variables used in revenue management. In the following, we will introduce these two forecasting approaches in more detail.

3.6 M-period Moving Average Forecasting

M-period moving average forecasting uses the terminology as presented in Chap. 3, Sect. 3.5 in a slightly different way. Nonetheless, the method as such directly builds on the ideas of ARMA processes, i.e., any value in y can be modeled by past values.

Let us assume that we want to forecast a future value of y at time $t + 1$. The M-period moving average forecast uses the mean of the previously M realized or forecasted values of the corresponding time series. In this context, M is called the span of the moving average. With $M = 3$ the corresponding forecasted value[9] for y at $t + 1$ is given by

$$\widehat{y}_{t+1} = \frac{y_t + y_{t-1} + y_{t-2}}{3}.$$

This can be easily rearranged for any value of M as follows

$$\widehat{y}_{t+1} = \frac{y_t + \ldots + y_{t-M+1}}{M}.$$

The moving average forecasting is a very simple and fast method, which requires limited computational capacities from a technical point of view. This makes it a suitable approach for forecasting in a revenue management context, where a substantial number of variables and flights need to be dealt with in parallel. The intuition behind moving average forecasting is quite simple: most recent observations serve as better predictors for the future than older values and data. At the same time, this is also the weakest point of this methodology, as the motivation behind it is rather heuristic and not economically founded incorporating any fundamental market dynamics.

Furthermore, the forecast itself will be exposed to more volatility and consequently less reliability, as the span decreases. Finally, if the data exhibits an upwards or downward

---

[9] Values with a hat represent estimated or forecasted values, while values without a hat denote realized and known observations.

trend, the moving average method leads to systematically biased results and wrong forecasts.

3.7 Exponential Smoothing

Exponential smoothing methods are among the most popular forecasting approaches in revenue management practice, as they are simple, robust, and lead to a reasonable forecast accuracy. Again, the concept itself is directly related to the mechanisms of the ARMA processes, as outlined in Chap. 3, Sect. 3.5.

As before, our aim is to forecast the future value of y at $t + 1$. Exponential smoothing weights the actual and the predicted outcome for y in period t in order to derive a value for $\hat{y}_{t+1}$. In mathematical terms, this can be written as

$$\hat{y}_{t+1} = \alpha y_t + (1 - \alpha)\hat{y}_t,$$

where $\hat{y}_t$ denotes the predicted value of y at time t and α is between zero and one determining the weight of actual and predicted values.

Similar to the steps we have taken in Chap. 3, Sect. 3.5 to derive the MA representation of the AR(1) process, we can substitute sequentially for $\hat{y}_t$ by shifting the equation in time, as it holds for any possible time period. This yields

$$\hat{y}_{t+1} = \alpha y_t + \alpha(1 - \alpha)y_{t-1} + (1 - \alpha)^2 \hat{y}_{t-1},$$

which again is a weighted average of exponentially decreasing past values with α steering the reaction of the forecast to recent and past values. This process of recursive substitution for predicted values of y can be repeated s times, which finally delivers the following relationship

$$\hat{y}_{t+1} = \alpha y_t + \alpha(1 - \alpha)y_{t-1} + \alpha(1 - \alpha)^2 y_{t-2} + \ldots + \alpha(1 - \alpha)^s y_{t-s} + (1 - \alpha)^{s+1} \hat{y}_0,$$

where $\hat{y}_0$ is the initial value.

In order to illustrate the dynamics of forecasting based on exponential smoothing, we have generated some arbitrary example data, which includes a trend. Furthermore, we have chosen α to be 0.5. The initial value for y has been set to 960, which is slightly above the actual realized value of 950. The results are depicted in Fig. 3.7. The black line shows the actual realized data, while the gray line describes the forecasted values obtained from the exponential smoothing approach. As we can see, the forecast follows the actual data movements of the original time series quite well. Nonetheless, the forecasted data follows the actual line with some delay, which is related to the fact that we have chosen a medium value for α and the entire forecast relies on past data.

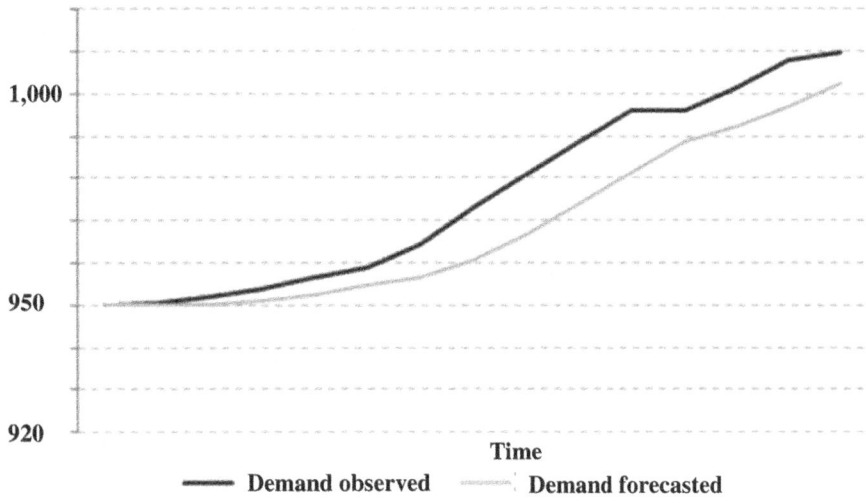

Fig. 3.7 Forecasting with exponential smoothing using example data with $\alpha = 0.5$

3.8 Checkpoint Chap. 3

This chapter has presented the cornerstones and major concepts of estimation and forecasting in revenue management. We have discussed the key theoretical elements and highlighted the mathematical foundations. The key topics from this chapter were:

- Motivation for unconstraining of revenue management data
- Introduction of the EM algorithm
- Static and dynamic forecasting
- Pick-up forecasting
- ARMA processes
- Moving average forecasting
- Exponential smoothing
  The reader should now be able to answer the following questions:

1. Why is unconstraining of data required in airline revenue management?
2. What is the difference between static and dynamic forecasting methods?
3. How does pick-up forecasting work in general?
4. What is the idea of ARMA processes and why are they useful in revenue management forecasting?
5. When will moving average forecasting lead to biased results?

Optimization, Types of Control, and Overbooking

4

As illustrated in Fig. 2.1, the optimization step takes place, after the forecasting has been done. It uses the corresponding results from forecasting to maximize the expected revenue of a flight.[1] Throughout this chapter, we will discuss the most relevant concepts of optimization in revenue management. This will finally allow us to understand the process flow of a standard revenue management system, as outlined in Chap. 2, Sect. 2.1, in all details. Furthermore, we will give a comprehensive introduction to overbooking approaches and their practical relevance. The chapter starts with an introduction, on how capacity is generally allocated and controlled in airline revenue management.

4.1 Booking Limits

Capacities in airline revenue management are generally steered and controlled through reservation classes. The availability of these reservation classes is constrained by corresponding booking limits. Typically, the reservation classes are denoted by the letters of the alphabet. This implies that in traditional revenue management 26 reservations classes are available for steering and controlling the inventory of a flight. Defining and conceptualizing the rules and conditions behind every reservation class and further behind every fare basis code, is the core task of pricing. In large airline organizations, particularly in network carriers, dedicated pricing departments will be assigned with this responsibility.

---

[1] In the case of network revenue management, the objective for revenue management might differ. Nonetheless, in the environment of leg-based revenue management the objective will be the revenue maximization on a single flight basis. Network revenue management will be discussed in detail throughout Chap. 5.

© Springer Fachmedien Wiesbaden GmbH, part of Springer Nature 2021
C. Cramer, A. Thams, *Airline Revenue Management*,
https://doi.org/10.1007/978-3-658-33721-6_4

In the following, we will primarily focus on revenue management and assume pricing to be kept separately, as it would go beyond the scope of this book.

In practice, booking limits are also referred to as AU, which stands for authorized capacity. Basically, we can distinguish between two different kinds of booking limits to constrain the amount of capacity that can be sold in any particular class at a given point in time.

Figure 4.1 explains these two approaches with simplified numerical examples. Let us first start with the case of partitioned booking classes, which distributes the available capacity into separate and independent blocks. The numerical example in Fig. 4.1 assumes a total available capacity of 30 units. These 30 units are allocated into four arbitrarily chosen reservation classes denoted by A, B, C, and D. Reservation class A has an availability of 5 units, B has 7 units, C has 10 units, and D has 8 units, which sums up to 30 units in total.

Let us suppose that 5 units are sold from class C. This will limit the net availability of class C to 5 units and the overall available capacity reduces from 30 to 25 units, while the availability of classes A, B, and D remains unchanged. This mechanism holds for all other classes accordingly, i.e., if a certain number of capacity is sold from class D, it will have no impact on the availability of the other classes, as partitioned booking classes or limits ensure independency concerning availability between each other.

In the case of nested booking limits or classes, the capacity allocation follows a pre-defined class hierarchy. The right-hand side of Fig. 4.1 depicts this approach. Again, the example assumes a total capacity of 30 units. Furthermore, reservation class A ranks highest in the hierarchy, followed by class B, C, and D, which ranks lowest. This class hierarchy has some implications. Opposite to the case of portioned booking classes, the total available capacity is now allocated to the reservation class with the highest hierarchy, i.e., class A. Again, let us now suppose that 5 units are sold from class C. Naturally, the total net availability reduces by 5–25 units. At the same time, the net availability for class C reduces by 5 units from 20 to 15 units. While in the partitioned case this decrease of net availability of class C had no impact on the other classes, the net availability of class D is now zero, as any transaction in higher ranked booking classes has an immediate impact on booking classes, which are lower in the class hierarchy. Hence, if booking classes follow a certain nesting, it also implies a dependency in terms of availability between the underlying reservation classes. As up to 25 passengers can book into class B, 5 seats will always be protected for the demand with the highest value in terms of willingness to pay in class A. Therefore, we can say that the protection level for class A amounts to 5 seats.

Both the partitioned and nested booking limit approaches have practical relevance. For example, imagine that we want to ensure that always 10 seats are available for crew proceedings. In this case, a portioned booking limit would allow to protect exactly 10 seats for this purpose regardless of the development of sales and net availabilities in other booking classes. A nested booking class allows to capture demand efficiently and effectively by reflecting different levels of willingness to pay along the nesting. Finally, combinations of the two approaches are frequently used in practice.

4.2 Littlewood's Rule

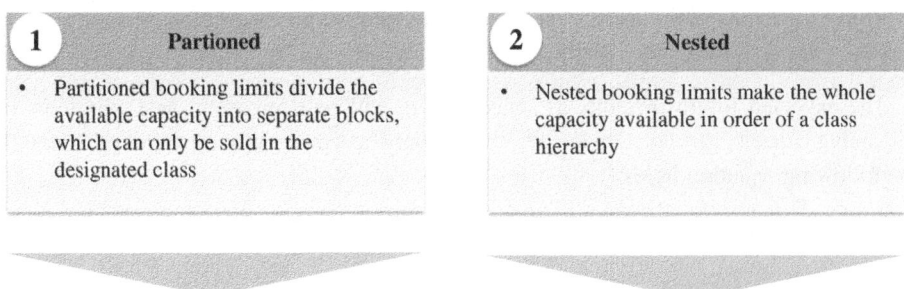

Fig. 4.1 Example of partitioned and nested booking classes

4.2 Littlewood's Rule

Throughout this section, we will introduce one of the earliest and simplest models to allocate capacities optimally to booking classes. The model goes back to Littlewood (1972).[2] Let us assume that we have only two classes, C_1 and C_2, with corresponding prices p_1 and p_2, where $p_1 > p_2$, and demand D_1 and D_2. C represents the total capacity. Furthermore, demand D_2 comes in first and is known and observable, while D_1 with the higher willingness to pay is random and will be only known at a later point in time.

From a revenue management perspective, the task is to decide, what capacity allocations for classes C_1 and C_2 lead to a maximization of revenues. If we were certain that the initially unknown and random demand for C_1 fills the total capacity, we would protect the entire capacity for D_1, which implies that the less valuable demand D_2 would be fully rejected. That means that the capacity allocation in terms of protections levels is fundamentally determined by the expected future demand for class 1. As D_1 is a random variable, we denote the underlying distribution by $F_1(\cdot)$. The solution to this simple optimization problem can be derived rather intuitively.

Let us suppose that we have an arbitrary number of x units of capacity remaining. We receive a request for class 2, which leads to the following two possible decisions:

1. Accept the request for class 2, which will lead to a revenue of p_2.

---

[2]Talluri and Ryzin (2005) offer an extended introduction into Littlewood's rule and other basic optimization approaches.

2. Reject the request for class 2, which will generate the expected future revenue $p_1 \cdot \text{Prob}(D_1 \geq x)$.

The expected future revenue, as stated above, will be decreasing, as x, the units of remaining capacity, grows. Obviously, we will only accept the request for class 2 now, if the following equation holds

$$p_2 \geq p_1 \text{Prob}(D_1 \geq x).$$

This equation implies that there will be an optimal protection level fulfilling the following two conditions

$$p_2 \leq p_1 Prob(D_1 \geq y_1^*)$$

$$p_2 > p_1 Prob(D_1 \geq y_1^* + 1),$$

where the second solution can be seen as a boundary solution in the sense that one additional unit of remaining capacity will make us accept the current request for class 2. If we further assume that demand for class 1 can be modeled by a continuous distribution denoted by $F_1(x)$, we can derive the optimal capacity allocation easily. For this purpose, we can rewrite the first condition as

$$p_2 = p_1 Prob(D_1 \geq y_1^*),$$

which yields

$$y_1^* = F_1^{-1}\left(1 - \frac{p_2}{p_1}\right).$$

F_1^{-1} represents the reverse function of the distribution function. This equation is known as Littlewood's rule giving an optimal protection level y_1^*. The corresponding booking limit is given by $b_2^* = C - y_1^*$.

In a nutshell, Littlewood's rule provides a formal framework to determine the optimal capacity allocation in a simple two-class environment. Intuitively, if the future expected demand decreases, the optimal capacity allocation will result in a lower protection level y_1^*. Oppositely, with increasing levels of future expected demand, we will impose lower booking limits b_2^*.

4.3 Expected Marginal Seat Revenue (EMSR)

The expected marginal seat revenue (EMSR) approach has a so-called a- and b-version, EMSR-a and EMSR-b. While EMSR-b has a higher practical relevance, the EMSR-a version, with a higher theoretical relevance, is able to explain the fundamental idea behind the approach, which is also directly related to Littlewood's rule. Therefore, we will focus on the EMSR-a throughout this introductory section.[3]

The EMSR-a belongs to the class of heuristic methods to compute optimal controls. From a practical point of view, the underlying heuristics are easy to run and code in a system environment. Therefore, the EMSR methodology is widely used within revenue management. The EMSR-a compares successively pairs of classes to determine the optimal protection levels for each of them. In the following, we will explain the mechanisms of EMSR-a in a rather intuitive way avoiding mathematical details as much as possible. This will allow readers with different analytical backgrounds to understand the basic mechanisms of EMSR-a. In Fig. 4.2, we apply the EMSR approach to a simple optimization problem with just two reservation classes.

The analysis, as shown in Fig. 4.2, is based on the following set of assumptions:

1. Two reservation classes C1 and C2
2. C2 has a price of €300, C1 of €400
3. Demand is stochastic and follows a time sequence, i.e., demand for C2 is known today, while demand for C1 will appear at a later point in time and hence is uncertain and stochastic.

The target is now to determine the optimal amount of seats to be protected for higher value demand or to put it differently: what is the optimal protection level for class 1? Again, as in the case of Littlewood's rule, we have two choices: we can either reject current demand for class C2, which would generate a certain and known revenue of €300 immediately, or we protect capacity for customers with a higher willingness to pay, as they would potentially pay a price of €400 at a later unknown point of time. That means we need to make a trade-off between accepting nonrandom, less valuable demand today and waiting for future random, more valuable demand.

Figure 4.2 gives a graphical solution to this problem. The x-axis denotes the capacity of up to a maximum of 189 seats. The y-axis represents the expected marginal seat revenue for selling one additional unit of capacity in the corresponding reservation class. As outlined in the assumptions, the demand for C2 is certain and known so that the marginal seat revenue amounts to €300 for all seats up to 189, which is reflected by the red line in Fig. 4.2. Further, we assume that demand for class 1 follows a normal distribution with a mean of 100 and a standard deviation of 10. This yields the blue line, which has a very simple interpretation. As on average we expect a demand of 100 passengers for class 1, it will be

---

[3]Talluri and van Ryzin (2005) offer a detailed overview of EMSR-b.

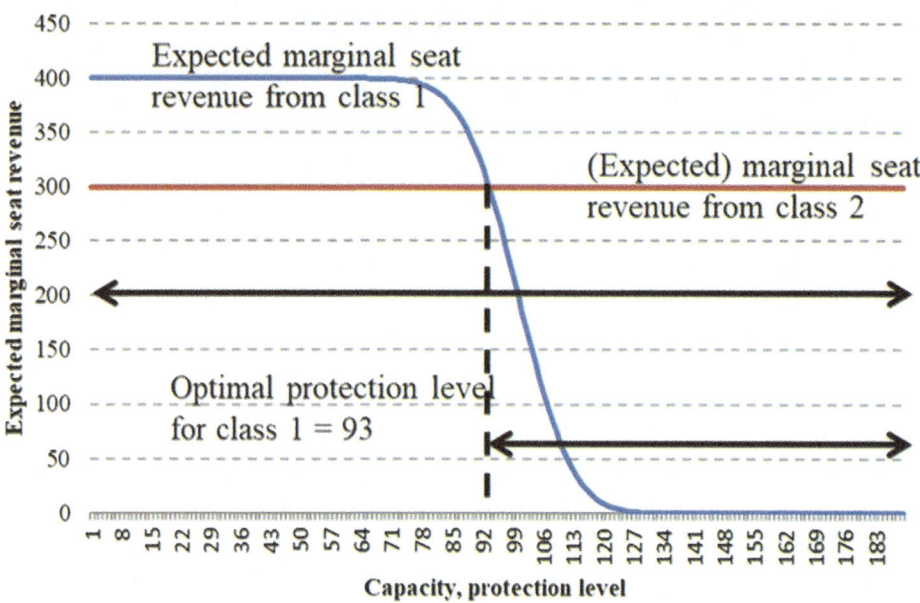

Fig. 4.2 Application of EMSR-a to determine the optimal set of controls in a two-class environment

very likely or almost certain that we will be able to sell one unit from class 1. Therefore, the expected marginal seat revenue, as represented by the blue line, has a value of around €400, which is the result of the probability of selling one unit in class 1 multiplied by the unit revenue for class 1. Also selling a second, third and fourth unit in class 1 is very likely, which makes the expected marginal seat revenue remain at a value of about €400 until we get into the interval of about 70 units of capacity, where the expected marginal seat revenue starts to decline. That means that the probability to sell one additional unit in class 1 becomes smaller. While this probability continues to decrease, the expected marginal seat revenue for class 1 equals €300 at exactly 93 units. This is where the blue line intercepts the red one. Therefore, it will be optimal to protect 93 units of capacity for class 1 in order to optimize the revenue in this example. Or to put it differently, in the case of nested booking classes the AU for class 2 would amount $189 - 93 = 96$ units and for class 1 it would be at 189, when overbooking effects are kept aside.

The EMSR-a can be extended to any arbitrary number of reservation classes, as the solution technique is similar. Figure 4.3 gives the graphical representation of the EMSR-a method for the case of three reservation classes.

Opposite to the case of only two reservation classes, as described above, we assume in Fig. 4.3 demand for all three reservation classes is random, as the curvature of the blue, red, and green lines indicates. As before, the intersection of the blue and red lines determines the optimal protection level for class 1, while the intersection of the red and green lines gives the optimal protection level for class 2. The black arrows in Fig. 4.3 indicate the corresponding AUs, which would result in the case of nested reservation classes.

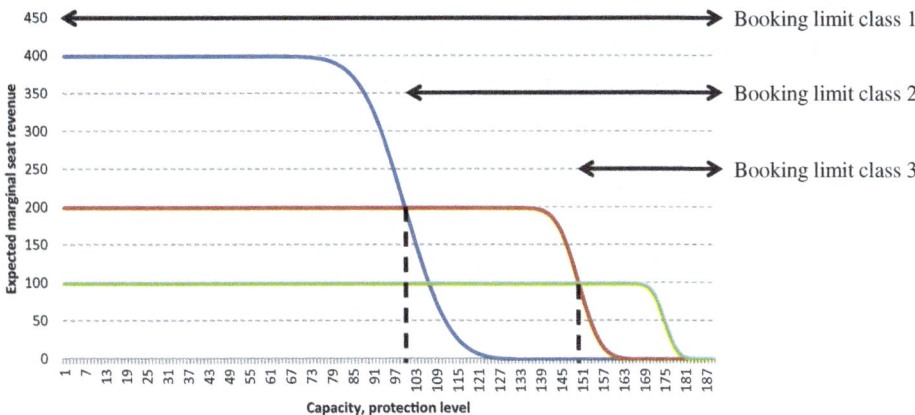

Fig. 4.3 EMSR-a extended to three booking classes

4.4 Overbooking

So far, we have implicitly assumed that the maximum AU of a flight exactly equals the total capacity of an aircraft, which means that overbooking does not take place. However, in practice, overbooking of flights is a frequently used instrument of revenue management to improve the economic performance of a flight. Therefore, overbooking can be a decisive lever for the overall profitability of an airline with the downside that it might negatively affect customer satisfaction, if the actual number of no-shows or cancelations is lower than expected, which results in denied boardings of passengers. In the following, we will explain the practical and commercial relevance of overbooking in more detail, before presenting different basic overbooking approaches. Finally, we will conclude with a brief overview of legal implications arising from the EU regulation 261.

4.5 Rationale for Overbooking

As already stated above, overbooking is an instrument to significantly improve the revenue performance of an airline. The reasons are related to the booking behavior of passengers, particularly

- Passengers cancel their bookings before the departure
- Passengers no-show for a flight
- Passengers make duplicate bookings.
- Passengers miss their connecting flights.
- Denied boarding costs may be lower than the expected revenue gain.
- Empty tour operator allotments

Obviously, passengers might cancel their booking before the planned departure so that overbookings are compensated by corresponding cancelations over time. The higher the number of expected cancelations will be, the more we can overbook a flight. Furthermore, some passengers might not cancel their booking actively, but will just not show up for a flight despite a valid booking. In addition, duplicate bookings on a flight are not unusual, e.g., as a result of technical problems, leading to no-shows on the day of departure. In a network carrier environment, people might miss their connecting flights due to operational problems causing no-shows accordingly. The costs for a denied boarding might be lower than the potential revenue gain. Imagine that on a strongly demanded flight the potential revenue per additional passenger is substantially higher than the costs for a denied boarding arising from rebooking, accommodation, etc. Finally, in practice, tour operators or any other B2B customer might hold allotments on a flight, which are frequently not fully filled offering the potential for overbookings.

In all these cases, overbookings contribute to an increase of load factor and revenue, while reducing the overall number of empty seats on a flight and consecutively throughout the entire network of an airline. Estimates indicate that overbookings can contribute to a revenue increase of up to 5%, of course depending on the actual no-show and cancelations rate in the airline network.[4] For touristic leisure airlines, the potential arising from overbooking will naturally be lower due to small cancelation and no-show rates among their customers than for a full network carrier focusing on business travelers, whose travel plans might change on a short-term notice.

Besides the upside revenue potentials arising from overbookings, it is crucial to keep in mind that every customer denied for boarding due to an overbooked aircraft will usually have a tremendously poor customer experience and satisfaction. Particularly, in the era of online distribution and social media, these negative impacts on customer satisfaction will often be transparent and visible to the public and other potential customers through platforms like TripAdvisor and Zoover or through Facebook, Instagram, LinkedIn, or TikTok. This can lead to an overall reputational damage for the entire company and its brand with substantial hidden and non-observable costs. In order to minimize this risk, it will be essential to implement proper and effective passenger handling processes in close collaboration with the operational units of an airline, particularly Ground Operations, when overbookings are done actively as part of capacity steering. Furthermore, every passenger, who is unable to board the aircraft, will trigger costs for alternative transportation, hotel accommodation, etc., which lowers the commercial benefits of overbooking. We will talk in more detail about the potential cost impacts of overbooking in the context of EU Regulation 261 in Sect. 4.9.

Table 4.1 shows the actual number of denied boardings for selected U.S. marketing carriers during the third quarter of 2019. The numbers are categorized by voluntary denied boardings, i.e., passengers, who gave up their seat on an oversold flight in exchange for

---

[4]Cf. Talluri and van Ryzin (2005).

compensation, and involuntary denied boardings, i.e., passengers, who wanted to travel, but were unable as a result of overbooking. The airlines are ordered by the rate of involuntary denied boardings per 10,000 passengers as given in the last column. On average, 0.19 involuntary denied boardings per 10,000 passengers have been reported, while American Airlines ranks at the top with a value of 0.68 denied boardings per 10,000 passengers. Overall, the number of voluntary denied bookings are substantially higher with an average value of 5.31 per 10,000 passengers showing that the largest fraction of denied boardings is handled through well-defined compensation and rebooking processes prior to departure. While Delta Air Lines shows the highest number of total denied boardings, it only reports three involuntary cases, which highlights the relevance of efficient and effective customer handling and complaint processes, when applying overbooking as part of revenue management. This typically includes a customer-centric process when selecting, which customers are to be denied for boarding. Furthermore, a well-elaborated process will help to reduce direct costs from denied boarding, while positively affecting customer satisfaction at the same time.

4.6 Deterministic Overbooking Approach

A core task of revenue management is to determine the optimal AU, when considering no-shows and cancelations. Let us assume that q denotes the constant probability that a customer with an existing booking finally shows up at the day and time of departure. Accordingly, $1-q$ is the probability that a passenger either cancels or no-shows for the flight.[5] This yields that in this deterministic environment the average show demand is exactly equal to the total capacity. In mathematical terms we obtain

$$AU_{opt} = \frac{C}{q}.$$

This approach is obviously very simplistic but offers in practice an intuitive way to get a first approximate result for the size of overbookings. Nonetheless, the approach is to be used with caution. As the equation indicates, AU_{opt} is a point-estimate for the optimal AU on a single flight. In reality, the actual q will be stochastic and fluctuate around a mean. Let us suppose that q is a normally distributed random variable with mean μ_q and standard deviation σ_q. That means that in 50% of the cases the actual cancelation and no-show rate will be higher than the average leading to denied boarding, while in 50% of the cases with the actual cancelation and no-show rate being lower than the average we will have empty seats on our flight. Therefore, this approach, which does not consider any stochastic

---

[5] In reality, q is rather a function of time than a static time-independent value. For the sake of simplicity, we neglect the impact of time on the probability of a passenger to cancel or no-show.

Table 4.1 Denied boarding by marketing carrier, scheduled domestic flights, and international flights originating in the U.S., July–September 2019

Marketing carrier	Denied boarding Voluntary	Involuntary	Enplaned passengers	Denied boarding per 10,000 pax Voluntary	Involuntary
Hawaiian Airlines Network	37	–	2,884,639	0.13	0
Delta Air Lines	46,408	3	50,701,859	9.15	0
United Airlines	20,702	15	38,738,623	5.34	0
Allegiant Air	135	2	3,836,145	0.35	0.01
Jetblue Airways	785	8	9,760,018	0.8	0.01
Spirit Airlines	4656	64	8,390,833	5.55	0.08
Southwest Airlines	4806	314	40,777,514	1.18	0.08
Alaska Airlines	3430	152	12,390,436	2.77	0.12
Frontier Airlines	893	230	5,731,264	1.56	0.4
American Airlines	37,367	3481	51,398,398	7.27	0.68
Total	119,219	4269	224,609,729	5.31	0.19

Source: Air Travel Consumer Report, Office of Aviation Enforcement and Proceedings, December 2019

impacts, will usually lead to significant operational challenges, as in 50% of the cases the average show demand will be higher than the available capacity. This finally leads to a suboptimal cost position concerning denied boarding compensations.

4.7 Stochastic Overbooking Approach

Belobaba et al. (2016) provide an augmented version of the static overbooking approach to allow the actual no-show rate to be uncertain, as it is the case in real-world applications. With this approach, we incorporate uncertainty about future no-show rates assuming the no-show rates to be represented by a normal distribution.

The idea is to find the AU, which will keep denied boarding to some predefined target level in the event that the flight is fully booked. As an example, we want to keep denied boardings at zero with a confidence of 95%, given by a statistical confidence interval. With estimated values for the random variable q and its underlying standard deviation σ_q the optimal AU can be calculated as follows:

$$AU_{opt} = \frac{C}{q + 1.645\sigma_q},$$

where 1.645 denotes the standardized normal value for a one-tailed 95% confidence interval implying that the objective of the airline would be to keep denied boardings at zero with 95% confidence. The more uncertain the number of no-shows is, the larger the denominator will be, as σ_q increases, which lowers the optimal AU. Intuitively, this means that more fluctuating no-show rates will lead to less aggressive overbooking policies and vice-versa.

To illustrate the mechanisms of this equation, let us assume the following numerical example: the capacity amounts to 100 seats, q equals 0.8 corresponding to a 20% no-show and cancelation rate. The underlying standard deviation equals 0.08 and the airline wants to keep denied boardings at zero with a confidence of 95%. Again, 1.645 is the z-value from the standard-normal distribution. Plugging in for the variables delivers the following results

$$AU_{opt} = \frac{100}{0.8 + 1.645 \times 0.08} \approx 107.34.$$

That means that the optimal AU amounts 107, which implies that we allow for an overbooking of up to seven passengers. A standard deviation of 0.1 would result in an optimal AU of approximately 103 showing the impact of rising uncertainty on the magnitude of overbookings. Furthermore, if the airline is indifferent between having denied boardings or not (50% confidence), the corresponding z-value will be zero and the stochastic overbooking approach is identical to the static approach described in Sect. 4.6.

4.8 Cost-based Overbooking Approach

The overbooking methods presented so far did not incorporate any cost elements. However, in reality, denied boarding can cause substantial costs as already briefly described in Sect. 4.5. In the following, we will derive the cost-based overbooking approach, which relies on a rather intuitive mathematical fundament.

Generally, in overbooking decisions, we face two kinds of costs, i.e., costs of denied boarding and costs of spoilage. The costs of denied boarding are obvious, as customers, whose boarding is denied, are entitled to obtain, e.g., hotel accommodation, an alternative flight or denied boarding compensation, etc. Hence, costs of denied boarding are a consequence of too aggressive overbooking. But also, a too conservative overbooking policy induces costs. These costs are referred to as costs of spoilage. They can be thought of as being opportunity costs. Imagine that an airline decides not to apply overbooking at all so that the maximum booking count on a flight equals its total capacity. As over time, this airline will experience some no-shows or cancelations among its passengers, some of the fully booked flights will depart with empty seats. Overbooking reduces the number of these empty seats, increasing revenues throughout the network, which in turn have the character of opportunity costs. Costs of spoilage and costs of denied boarding show in different directions. While costs of spoilage decrease with growing AU, denied boarding costs

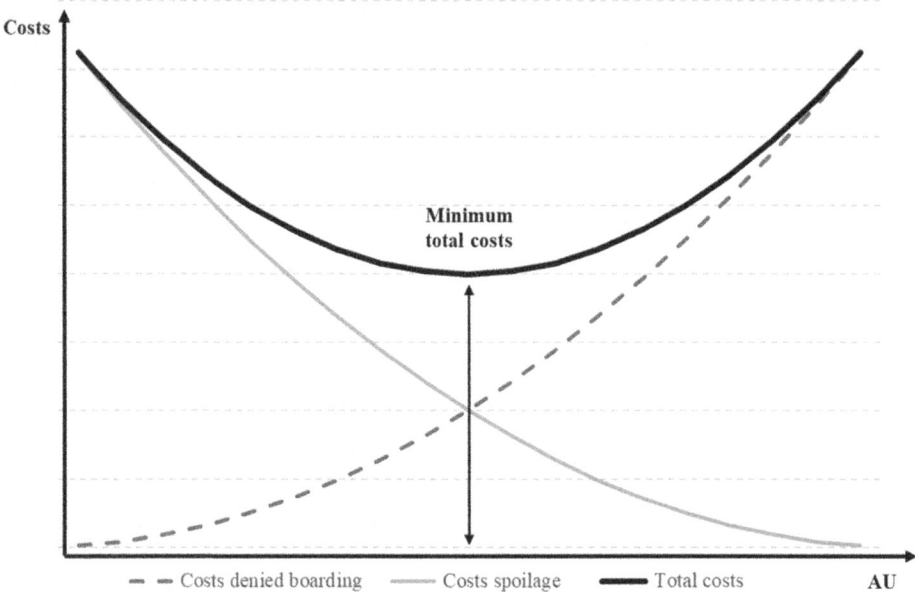

Fig. 4.4 Graphical representation of the cost-based overbooking approach

increase. Therefore, the objective of cost-based overbooking is to minimize the total sum of costs of denied boarding and costs of spoilage by allocating the optimal AU.

Figure 4.4 gives the general pattern of the two cost components in overbooking including the view of resulting total costs. In this case, at the intersection of the two curves, the total costs are minimized determining the optimal AU. The slope of the denied boarding costs curve is naturally given by the size of direct denied boarding costs and the expected no-show rate, while the slope of the costs of spoilage curve depends on the expected spot rate for the flight and again on the expected no-show rate.

4.9 Legal Implications: EU Regulation 261

The costs associated with overbooking and flight irregularities, in general, have substantially increased in recent years. The reason for this is that several countries have introduced legal regulations, which oblige airlines to compensate passengers in the case of denied boarding or significant flight irregularities. The Regulation (EC) No 261/2004 defines rules on compensation and assistance to passengers in the event of denied boarding, flight cancelations, or long delays of flights for all airlines registered in the EU and non-EU airlines departing from an airport within the EU. The compensation per passenger amounts to €250 up to €600 depending on the geographical distance of the corresponding flight. The flight distances defining the size of compensation payments are categorized into three groups:

1. A flight of less than 1500 km in distance: €250 cash compensation
2. A flight within the EU of greater than 1500 km in distance, or any other flight of greater than 1500 km but less than 3500 km in distance, €400 cash compensation
3. A flight not within EU of greater than 3500 km in distance: €600 cash compensation

Furthermore, a passenger is entitled to obtain in any of the three groups of flight distances:

- Repayment of the cost of unused flight tickets, and for used tickets where the flight (s) taken no longer serve(s) any purpose in relation to the passenger's original travel plan, and where applicable, a flight back to the original point of departure at the earliest opportunity
- Rerouting under similar conditions to the intended final destination at the earliest opportunity
- Rerouting under similar conditions to the intended final destination at the passenger's leisure, subject to the availability of seats

Obviously, the costs of denied boarding increase substantially lowering the net commercial benefits of overbooking. Hence, when applying a cost-based overbooking approach, which incorporates the effects arising from such legal requirements, the general overbooking will deliver more conservative results than the other approaches presented earlier throughout this chapter.

4.10 Checkpoint Chap. 4

In this chapter, we have looked at the fundamentals of optimization including overbooking. In particular, we have introduced Littlewood's rule as the working horse of optimization in revenue management. Furthermore, we have illustrated the concept of EMSR as a key method to derive the optimal capacity allocation. The key topics from this chapter were

- Nested and partitioned booking limits
- Littlewood's rule
- Expected marginal seat revenue (EMSR) version a and b
- Deterministic overbooking approach
- Stochastic overbooking approach
- Cost-based overbooking approach

The following questions should now be easy to answer:

1. What are the differences between nested and portioned booking limits? What could be potential practical use cases for one or the other?
2. What is the implication and interpretation of Littlewood's rule?
3. Explain the core mechanisms in EMSR to derive the optimal capacity allocation in a two and three-class environment.
4. Describe and explain the main rationale for applying cost-based overbooking approaches.
5. What are the deficiencies of deterministic overbooking methods?

Network Revenue Management 5

In the previous chapters, we have worked with pure leg-based revenue management techniques, which are typically used in regional and low-cost airlines with a low share of connecting passengers in their network and mostly point-to-point offers. However, major network carriers operate complex hub-and-spoke networks, where customers can choose and book connections from their origin to destination (O&D) with a stopover at a hub airport. The hub consolidates demand from various airports, which are connected to the hub airport by different connecting flights.

5.1 Pros and Cons of Network Revenue Management

Figure 5.1 illustrates the basic principles of a hub-and-spoke network. In this example, New York and Zurich act as hubs within the network connected to various airports such as Hamburg, Berlin, Geneva, Rome, Seattle, or Portland. Customers obtain a wider range of product offers. While a point-to-point carrier would only offer flights between single airports, e.g., from Hamburg to Zurich or Miami to New York, a network carrier offers Hamburg to New York or Hamburg to Seattle to the market with stopovers in Zurich and New York.

As explained above, the methodologies and approaches we have discussed so far aim to maximize revenue on a single flight. However, they are not necessarily able to maximize revenues in a complex O&D network carrier environment. While network revenue management can be an instrument to lever additional revenue, it has the downside that it will certainly add significant additional complexity to the core commercial processes along the value chain of an airline. Particularly planning, scheduling, and pricing will be substantially affected by the change from a leg-based to a network-based commercial setup. Naturally, it will require an attractive schedule, which is operationally feasible, to generate

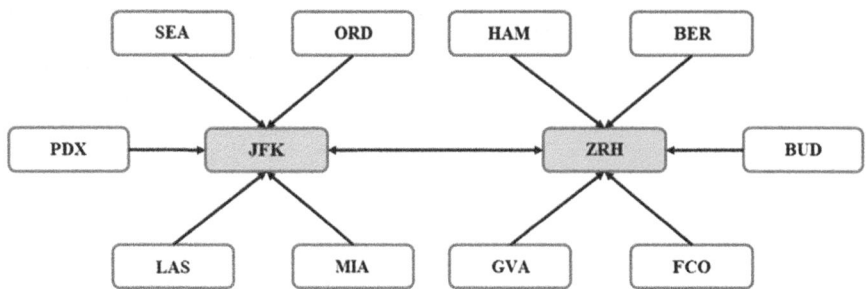

Fig. 5.1 Schematic overview of a hub-and-spoke network with New York and Zurich as hub airports

a sufficient number of connecting passengers. Besides further organizational challenges, network revenue management requires more data, which needs to be collected, managed, and finally stored within the corresponding systems widely changing the system landscape of revenue management. As the number of O&D and accordingly products on sale increase all major steps in revenue management become more challenging and complex, as both the number of forecasts and optimizations grow overproportionally.

The revenue gain of network revenue management comes with the price of complexity. Therefore, a relevant number of connecting passengers within the network is needed to gain a positive net effect from changing to this more complex commercial setup. Airlines with a low share of connecting passengers will typically have very limited positive revenue effects from the introduction of network revenue management techniques. Nonetheless, properly applied network revenue is expected to generate between 1.5 and 3% additional revenues in comparison to leg-based revenue management.[1]

5.2 The Fundamentals of Network Revenue Management

In the following, we will illustrate the basic mechanisms of network revenue management based on some simple numeric examples. Our target will be to maximize the total network revenue.

Let us assume that an airline offers the O&D Las Vegas (LAS) to Zurich (ZRH) with a stopover in New York (JFK), as already given in Fig. 5.2.

Figure 5.2 describes the itinerary including the underlying legs A and B. Each leg can be booked separately, while at the same time a passenger can book legs A and B combined as a multi-leg flight. Obviously, a booking on leg A will limit the availability for potential O&D demand from Las Vegas to Zurich, as the seat will be taken by a single-leg passenger. Of course, the same is true for a single booking on leg B.

---

[1] Cf. Talluri and van Ryzin (2005).

5.2 The Fundamentals of Network Revenue Management

Fig. 5.2 Las Vegas to Zurich as an example of a simple O&D problem

Furthermore, we assume that there are only two booking classes C1 and C2, where C1 is the more valuable class. With two classes and three possible O&Ds, leg A, leg B and the corresponding multi-leg flight, a customer can choose from six possible products A1, A2, B1, B2, AB1, AB2, where the numbers denote the respective booking class.[2] This also highlights the increasing complexity of network revenue management indicated by the growing number of possible products offered to the market. This additional complexity will only lead to a commercial net benefit, if the newly created products AB1 and AB2 generate significant market demand. Let us further assume that LAS-JFK has exactly one seat left, which means we have the choice between the following two alternatives:

1. Use the remaining seat for point-point traffic, i.e., LAS-JFK
2. Use the remaining seat for a connecting passenger from LAS to ZRH.

We suppose that the airline receives two requests for these seats. The first request is for leg A from LAS to JFK at a price of €400, which corresponds to class C1. The second request is for the O&D from LAS to ZRH at €560, which is matched by class C2. Let us now intuitively derive the solution.

In a leg-based revenue management environment, the more valuable demand from a single flight perspective is served first, i.e., C1. That means that the seat will be used for serving the passenger traveling from LAS-JFK. This option will generate an earned revenue of €400, while obviously, the load factor on JFK-ZRH remains unchanged.

When applying the rationales of network revenue management, the decision will be different, as the demand maximizing the earned network revenue will be served first. As a result, the last remaining seat will be used for a transit passenger from Las Vegas to Zurich with a corresponding revenue of €560.

Belobaba et al. (2016) state that generally revenue maximization over a network of connecting flights thus requires two different strategies, under different conditions. The airline should try to increase availability to high-revenue passengers, e.g., for long-haul flights, regardless of the underlying yield per passenger, when empty seats are likely on the relevant legs along the requested itinerary. On the other hand, if the corresponding legs are expected to be fully booked, the airline should reject low-yield demand for connecting passengers and rather focus on point-to-point demand in order to maximize revenue across its network.

---

[2] Cf. Klein and Steinhardt (2008).

5.3 Revenue Value Buckets

The application of network revenue management requires a different solution for capacity controls. The instruments of capacity control, as described in Chap. 4, Sect. 4.1, will have substantial limitations, as they do not allow to differentiate O&D requests by value. One of the first and simplest approaches to overcome this problem in network revenue management is the introduction of so-called revenue value buckets.[3] Revenue value buckets disentangle the static relationship between a booking class and a fare type. The idea of revenue value buckets can be best illustrated by using a simple numeric example. Following Belobaba et al. (2016) we assume that we have five booking classes Y, B, M, Q, and V with Y having the highest fare on a particular leg and V having the lowest. Further, we use the example shown in Fig. 5.2 augmented by an additional O&D from LAS to CAI (Cairo) via JFK. The basic idea is to assign each fare type on a particular O&D to a comparable fare type on another O&D through a simple and static mapping process using virtual fare classes. The actual seat availability for an O&D finally depends on the availability of the corresponding revenue value buckets on each leg of the itinerary, which the passenger wants to book.

The upper part of Table 5.1 shows the corresponding fares on an O&D basis. In the lower part of Table 5.1, the resulting virtual class mapping for a given grid of upper and lower fare values is shown.

Each virtual class contains those booking classes with a comparable monetary value defined by the lower and upper limits. For instance, the B class for LAS-JFK and the V class for LAS-CAI both are assigned to virtual class 8. Hence, virtual class 8 groups different booking classes. Furthermore, the Y class for LAS-JFK is assigned to virtual class 7, while the Q class for LAS-ZRH is assigned to virtual class 6, which implies a higher seat availability for LAS-ZRH, as the total revenue value is larger than for LAS-JFK despite the nominal higher ranking of the reservation class. At his point, it is important to notice that the virtual classes are not visible to the outside world and represent a purely internal airline view. Of course, the introduction of virtual fare classes requires some technical capabilities within the system landscape of an airline. Also, on the commercial side setting up and maintaining such a mapping process as outlined above adds complexity and transaction costs to sales and marketing processes.

The rather simple revenue bucket approach has the downside to bias capacity allocations toward O&Ds with longer distances, as they generate a higher overall revenue contribution throughout the network. Hence, connecting passengers tend to be served first, even in cases where point-to-point traffic might yield preferential economic results. In our example, the leg from LAS to JFK will bear displacement costs, whenever this flight is used for connecting passengers traveling to either CAI or ZRH. In the following, we will introduce

---

[3] Cf. Belobaba et al. (2016).

5.4 Displacement Costs

Table 5.1 Revenue buckets derived from virtual class mapping

Class	LAS-JFK	LAS-ZRH, via JFK	LAS-CAI, via JFK
Fare oneway in €			
Y	520	1250	1500
B	390	1000	1100
M	250	790	850
Q	180	650	700
V	90	300	360
Virtual class	Lower limit	Upper limit	Mapping
1	1351	1500	Y LAS-CAI
2	1201	1350	Y LAS-ZRH
3	1051	1200	B LAS-CAI
4	901	1050	B LAS-ZRH
5	751	900	M LAS-ZRH, M LAS-CAI
6	601	750	Q LAS-ZRH, Q LAS-CAI
7	451	600	Y LAS-JFK
8	301	450	B LAS-JFK, V LAS-CAI
9	151	300	Q LAS-JFK, M LAS-JFK, V LAS-ZRH
10	1	150	V LAS-JFK

a virtual nesting approach, which incorporates potential costs of displacement on certain legs.

5.4 Displacement Costs

An application and implementation of standard revenue buckets, as outlined in Sect. 5.3, can lead to suboptimal capacity allocations, as impacts, particularly on shorter legs within an O&D, are not taken into account. Therefore, it can be essential to incorporate the impact of displacement costs on certain legs as part of the capacity allocation mechanism. As before, we make use of a virtual class mapping, which we will augment by expected downline leg displacement costs.

Let us again use the numerical example given in Table 5.1. The fare amount for the M class from LAS to ZRH equals €790. The standard revenue bucket approach suggests a revenue contribution of the same size for the entire network. Let us further assume that there is high demand for the point-to-point flight from LAS to JFK leading to displacement costs of €500. In this case, the net revenue contribution generated from a passenger booking an itinerary in M class from LAS to ZRH amounts to €290. The M class from LAS to ZRH, previously mapped under virtual class 5, will now be assigned to virtual class 9 leading to a substantially lower seat availability.

This example illustrates how a correction mechanism for displacements costs works in general. Particularly, in cases where there is a high demand on local flights, e.g., due to a trade fair, school holidays, etc., adjusting for displacement costs will be crucial in order to obtain optimal results.

5.5 Bid Price Control

An airline will accept a request if the revenue value of an itinerary minus the downline revenue displacement cost is larger than the value of the last seat on a single leg.[4] In mathematical terms, this can be expressed as follows

Revenue value − displacement cost > value of last available seat on a leg.

This can be easily rewritten as

Revenue value > value of last available seat on a leg + displacement cost.

The sum of the value of the last available seat on a leg and the corresponding displacement cost represents the bid price for an O&D. Hence, we finally obtain the following relationship

Revenue value > minimum acceptable bid price.

This concept is also known as bid price control, which is one of the most prominent concepts in network revenue management. In the following, we use a simple two-leg example to illustrate the mechanisms of bid price control. Again, let us assume that a customer requests a seat from LAS to ZRH via JFK. The bid price for the leg from LAS to JFK amounts to €250, while the bid price for the leg from JFK to ZRH equals €650. That results in a total bid price for LAS to ZRH of €900. Using the values given in Table 5.1, yields that booking classes B and Y are available preventing low-yield connecting passengers displace yieldable point-to-point demand.

5.6 Checkpoint Chap. 5

This chapter has covered and introduced the basics of network revenue management. Besides the overall motivation for network revenue management, we have addressed the concepts of revenue value buckets and displacement cost in a network carrier environment.

---

[4]Cf. Belobaba et al. (2016).

5.6 Checkpoint Chap. 5 59

Finally, we have derived the frequently used approach of bid price control. Furthermore, we have briefly described the general challenges and caveats of network revenue management. In particular, we have introduced the following approaches

- Hub-and-spoke networks
- Fundamentals and motivation of network revenue management
- Revenue value buckets
- Displacement cost
- Bid price control

The following questions should now be easy to answer:

1. What is the aim of network revenue management? What are the challenges?
2. How do revenue value buckets generally work?
3. What is the motivation of displacement cost? How are they linked to the concept of revenue value buckets?
4. Please describe the relationship between bid price control on the one hand and displacement cost on the other hand.

Ancillary Revenues 6

The global market share of low-cost carriers offering no-frills products to their customers with the opportunity to book additional product and service components has been growing from 15.7% in 2006 to 31% in 2019.[1] This shows the constantly growing relevance of low-cost carriers from both a demand and supply side, while airlines with traditional business models keep losing market shares and partially adopt certain components of low-cost carriers, particularly in the field of additionally bookable product and service components. A recent survey among the U.S. American customers in 2019 revealed that for 57% the ticket price is a crucial aspect when buying an airline ticket for personal travel, which makes price the most important criterion when choosing a flight.[2] For decades, we can observe an overall negative price trend in the market despite various attempts of airlines to raise prices. The average return airfare before surcharges and taxes in 2017 was estimated at $351, which was 63% below 1995 levels,[3] while the global airline market kept growing until 2019.

As a result of declining ticket revenues, we see a substantial increase in ancillaries revenues arising from sales of additional products and services, which can be basically grouped into flight-related and non-flight-related offers. The actual development is depicted in Fig. 6.1, showing more than a tripling of global ancillary revenues in less than a decade. A fraction of these ancillary revenues was included in the base ticket fare in the past explaining a part of the decrease of ticket revenues, as airlines have stripped down their standard product offers excluding product components such as meals, baggage, or seat reservations. While this might appear like a pure change in accounting methodologies, it

---

[1] Cf. Statista (2019a).
[2] Cf. Statista (2019b).
[3] Cf. IATA (2016).

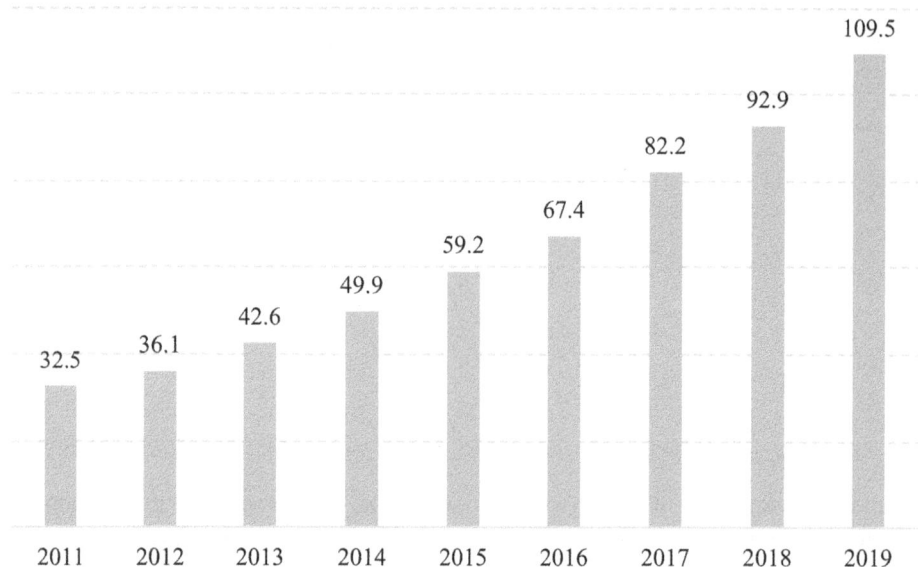

Fig. 6.1 Total ancillary revenue in the airline industry from 2011 to 2020 (in billion U.S. dollars). (Source: Statista / Ideaworks)

also highlights the change in product offers driven by the overall high importance of prices when it comes to customer decisions, as stated above.

Figure 6.2 shows the return on invested capital for the two business models low-cost carrier and network carrier for the time period 2004 till 2011 by region. Across all geographic regions, low-cost carriers significantly outperform network carriers in terms of return on invested capital, e.g., by up to 4 percentage points for the case of Europe, indicating the corresponding market success of the low-cost carrier business model, which is closely linked to a wide offer of ancillary products and services.

Figure 6.3 depicts the airlines with the highest ancillary revenue as a share of total revenue in 2019. The U.S.-based low-cost carriers Spirit Airlines and Allegiant rank at the top with an ancillary revenue share of more than 45%, which emphasizes the importance of ancillary sales in the overall commercial strategy of low-cost carriers.

Hence, ancillary revenues have become a crucial ingredient for the profitability of an airline, which in turn has an impact on the sales and distribution approach of the airline industry with retailing approaches gaining importance. To put it differently, many airlines would not be profitable without the generation of solid ancillary revenues.

IATA (2013) has analyzed the relationship between airline profitability and ancillary revenues. The analysis categorizes the different revenue components by airfare, ancillary revenues, cargo, and other revenues to compare the revenue stream with the overall cost block broken down on a per passenger basis. Table 6.1 gives the numerical results of this analysis. In 2012, approximately $12 per passenger was generated by sales of ancillary

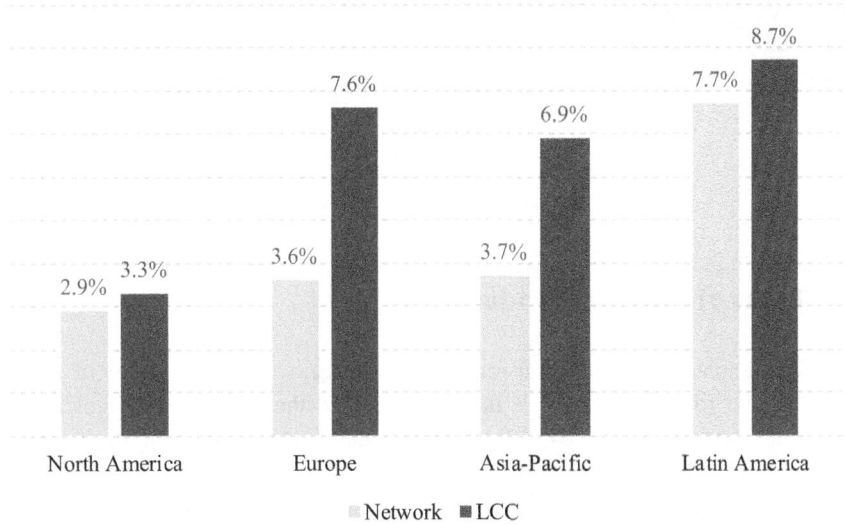

Fig. 6.2 Return on invested capital by region, 2004–2011. (Source: IATA 2013)

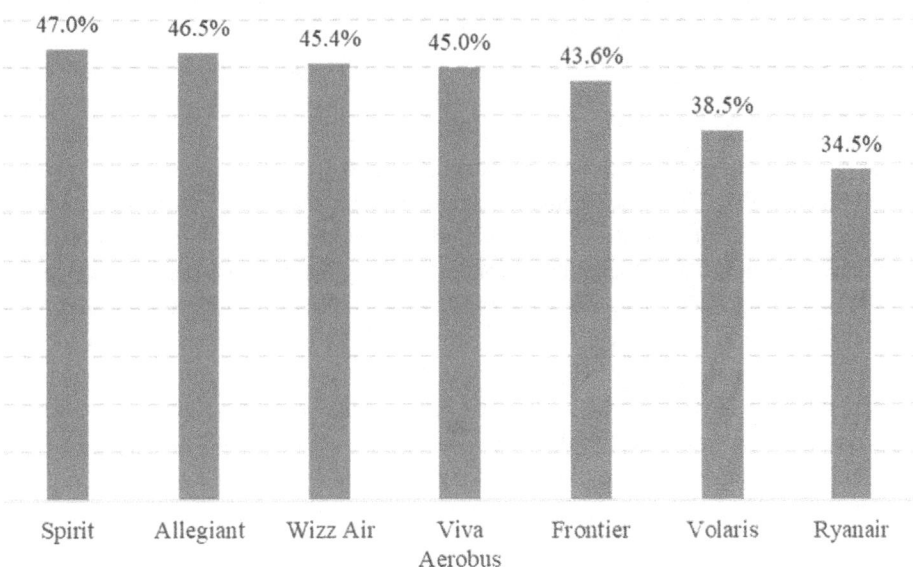

Fig. 6.3 Airlines with the highest ancillary revenue as a share of total revenue in 2019, source: IdeaWorks

products. The total net profit per passenger amounted to $2.56, which implies that airlines on a global basis would have been unprofitable without the generation of ancillary revenues making them an integral part of modern airline revenue streams.

Table 6.1 Worldwide airline financial results per departing passenger, USD, 2012

	Revenues	Costs	Net profit
Airfare	181.91	–	=
Ancillary	12.09		
Cargo & other	34.26		
Total	228.26	225.7	2.56

Source: IATA (2013)

6.1 Types of Ancillary Products

The previous explanations have illustrated the growing overall importance of ancillary revenues. In the following, we will further categorize the different types of ancillary products and services, which will allow for a better understanding of the underlying commercial business model.

In recent years, airlines have become very creative in designing and offering new ancillary product types. With the market entry of low-cost carriers, airlines started to generate ancillary revenues from unbundling the traditional flight product into separate components. Product components such as baggage, seat reservations, or meals were excluded from the base fare, which allowed to calculate with lower base prices in a highly competitive market environment, where prices are the most decisive factor in the marketing funnel. In the meanwhile, airlines have substantially extended their range of ancillary product offers to other segments of the touristic value chain.

The U.S.-based carrier Allegiant, as shown in Fig. 6.3, exhibits an ancillary revenue share of almost 50%. The reader is highly recommended to check the website of Allegiant, as it gives an excellent impression of the underlying commercial strategy, which leads to this remarkably high share of ancillary revenues.[4] Throughout the customer journey on the website of Allegiant, the customer can choose from a variety of flight-related and non-flight-related products and services ranging from baggage, seat reservation, hotel accommodation over rental cars to credit cards. The British airline Jet2[5] runs a similar retail strategy, which is closely linked to the own in-house tour operator Jet2holidays, which offers package holidays on Jet2 flights. The German airline Eurowings[6] is a good example for offering pre-bundled fare families to customers, which allows passengers to select from a set of different product bundles, which fulfills the needs of different customer segments.

In Fig. 6.4, we see a schematic categorization of possible ancillary revenue sources. Basically, we can differentiate between the core product, which is associated with the pure ticket revenue and other ancillary-product income. A modern airline sales and distribution landscape will also provide further unbundled product components like meals, priority

---

[4] www.allegiant.com.
[5] www.jet2.com.
[6] www.eurowings.com.

boarding, an upgrade into the next higher compartment, or different payment solutions resulting in credit card fees to its customers. Products and services in this category tend to be flight-related, which used to be part of the standard ticket in the past, as outlined above. In recent years, airlines have introduced an increasing number of non-flight-related products leading to commission-based ancillary revenues. In Fig. 6.4, this category of ancillary revenue sources is depicted by the outer gray circle. Examples of commissioned-based ancillary revenues are parking lots, which the airline markets on behalf of an airport, duty-free shopping, particularly when ordered in advance, or distribution of rental cars. However, the range and list of commissioned-based and non-flight-related ancillary offers are continuously growing, as airlines tend to establish new sources of ancillary revenues, while ticket revenues are continuously under pressure. Hence, the examples for commission-based ancillary revenues, given in Fig. 6.4, are not exhaustive but have to be understood as prominent use cases. Generally, the commercial focus of airlines on retailing combined with the extension of the product range will lead to a further increase in the relative importance of ancillary revenues in airline distribution.

6.2 Implications for Revenue Management

Traditional revenue management, as described in the previous chapters, focuses primarily on the maximization of ticket revenues. The growing share of ancillary revenues exposes classical revenue management to substantial challenges requiring a revised approach of capacity steering and allocation, which incorporates the impacts of ancillary revenues. In the following, we will elaborate on the implications for revenue management from an increasing relevance of ancillary revenues for airlines.

As outlined in Chap. 2, computerized revenue management systems have the target to maximize total revenue. In this context, total revenue refers to the ticket-based revenue, which is a declining fraction of total revenues, particularly in low-cost carrier environments, as explained earlier in this chapter. With the introduction of ancillary services and products, airlines have often split organizations and the corresponding price and revenue responsibility into a revenue management and a product unit. While revenue management units sign responsible for the ticket revenues, product units are accountable for the revenue streams arising from the sales of ancillary services and products. This can lead to conflicting targets across the organization, as an end-to-end transparency and an overall accountability for revenues are not necessarily given. On the one hand, revenue management will seek to maximize the unit revenue, i.e., RASK, based on ticket revenue by generating the optimal mix of load factor and ticket fare. On the other hand, a product department responsible for ancillary revenues will require passenger volumes in order to be able to lever its full potentials, as each additional passenger will potentially be a source for additional sales of ancillary products and services. This conflict of targets between product and revenue management can result in suboptimal commercial outcomes for the entire

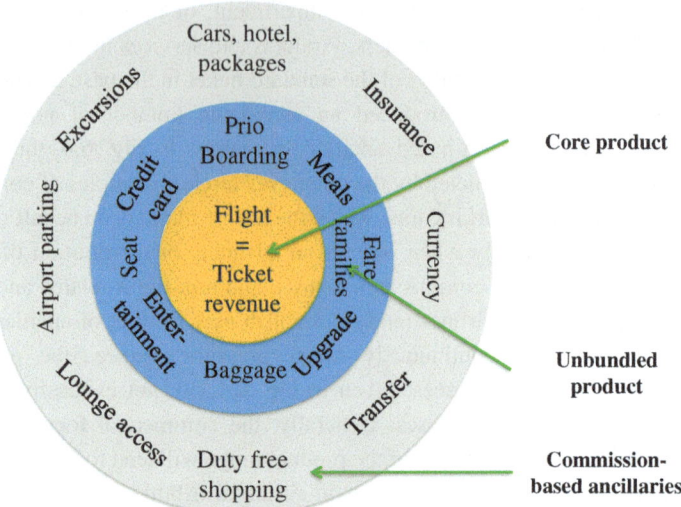

Fig. 6.4 Schematic categorization of ancillary revenue sources

company, particularly if each department is managed and measured separately and more or less independent from each other.

Hence, a modern and successful ancillary revenue management relies on a strong organizational linkage between classical revenue management and product management ensuring a transparent end-to-end view on revenue streams and potentials at any time. This also implies that the traditional role of a revenue manager fundamentally changes. While in the past, revenue managers have primarily focused on booking data and patterns in terms of volumes, revenues, compartments, etc., modern revenue management closely incorporates customer-oriented data. With the rise of online direct sales, customer data is widely available opposite to the early days of revenue management. This offers a wide range of commercial opportunities including a strict customer-centric sales approach of ancillary products based on quantitative data. Finally, this gives the opportunity to display specific and personalized offers to individual customers or customer segments.

Figure 6.5 gives a schematic overview of potential ancillary products and services, which an airline can offer to a customer at different points of time along the customer journey. The actual portfolio of product components finally depends on the customer profiles and segments within the route network of an airline. Leisure passengers will naturally have different product preferences than business travelers concerning baggage allowance or flexibility of a ticket. Again, the analysis and interpretation of customer data is a key lever to obtain a high conversion rate in selling ancillary products.

Furthermore, the conceptualization and introduction of new products is not only a pure commercial problem within an airline organization, as the implementation is finally with the operational departments, particularly Ground OPS. These units need to make sure that all product promises are delivered to the customers with the desired quality. Therefore, it is

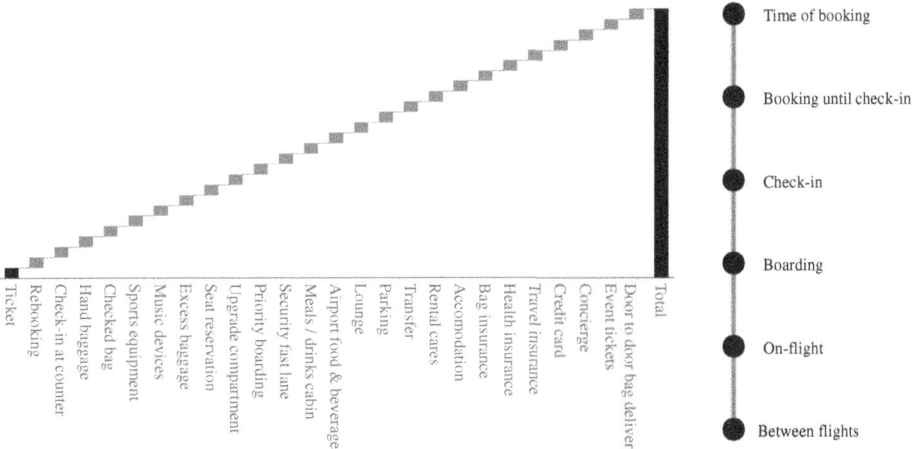

Fig. 6.5 Schematic revenue generation from product up-sell opportunities throughout the customer journey

essential that any change in the product specification is closely aligned and accompanied by the corresponding operational units, which finally sign responsible for the product delivery.

Figure 6.6 gives an impression of the product specification of Ryanair for its three fares types: Standard, Plus, and Flex Plus, each of them bundling specific product components. The base fare ("Standard") only includes a small baggage item, while both carry-on and check-in baggage have to be purchased as part of the ancillary product offer. Rebooking or cancellation is not possible in the base fare, while the Plus tariff offers rebooking and cancellation against a fee, as indicated in Fig. 6.6. Customizing and optimizing these product offers relies on data science approaches, which we will discuss and present in detail in Chap. 7.

6.3 Checkpoint Chap. 6

Throughout this chapter, we have introduced the principles of ancillary revenue management. We have discussed the historical development and the increasing importance of ancillary services and products for the overall income of an airline. Furthermore, we have highlighted organizational challenges arising from selling ancillary products and services. The key topics covered in this chapter were:

- Rationale and relevance of ancillary revenue management
- Types of ancillary revenues, services, and products
- Linkage between ticket and ancillary revenues
- Customer data and ancillary revenue management
- Levering ancillary revenues through data science

Fare type	Standard	Plus	Flex Plus	Characteristics
Small baggage item	40x20x25cm	Yes	Yes	• Standard fee without free carry-on baggage
Carry-on baggage	From €6 online €25 at airport (10kg / 55x40x20cm)	Yes (10kg)	Yes (10kg)	• Flex Plus without checked baggage, also not as ancillary
Airport counter check-in	No	No	Yes	• No F&B included in all fares
Checked-in baggage	$	20kg	No	• Discount for families on Baggage and ASR
Loyalty points	No	No	No	• Extra baggage as package with Priority Boarding
Rebooking	No	$	Yes	
Cancelation	No	$	Yes	
Priority boarding	$	Yes	Yes	
Fast Lane	$	$	Yes	
Seat reservation	$	Standard	Any row	
Food & beverage	$	No	No	

Fig. 6.6 Product specification by fare type, Ryanair, April 2020. (Source: Own analysis / www.ryanair.com)

6.3 Checkpoint Chap. 6

The reader should now be able to answer the following questions:

1. What are the reasons for the increasing importance of ancillary revenues?
2. Why is it important to ensure a strong organizational linkage between traditional revenue management and product departments?
3. What opportunities does data science offer, when it comes to ancillary revenue management?
4. To what extent does the role of a revenue manager change with the introduction of ancillary revenues?
5. How is the development of core commercial KPIs, such as yield per passenger and load factor, impacted, when ancillary revenues are incorporated?

Data Science and Revenue Management

7

"Being data-driven" has been touted by management consultants and the business press as a cure-all for business challenges for several years now. But what exactly does it mean? Any modern manager has access to a plethora of reports and dashboards that they happily use to point out their performance or the improvement needs of others.

We argue, however, that this is an inherently limited way of working: these reports allow the identification of past events. Their cause and even more so a recommended course of action in the future leave considerable room for interpretation and debate. The authors have experienced in many different organizations on their own how this interpretation of "data-driven" leads to inefficiencies, company politics, and wrong decisions.

The field of revenue management has—already decades ago—demonstrated a different approach, namely that of a scientific way of optimized operational decision-making which we subsume under the term "data science" in the remainder of this chapter.

While also being an often over- and misused technological term in recent years, data science has seen important practical improvements that enable business applications on a broad range of topics and with comparably low barriers to entry.

Some key reasons for this widespread adoption and lowered barriers to entry include:

- Methods employed in this field are more and more moving out of academia and into the public realm through a) open publication platforms such as arxiv.org and a successfully established open-source culture with github.com as a central resource, b) free industry-strength tooling (R, Python, Julia) with many specialized software packages for different application areas, and c) a vast amount of free and paid training offerings (edX, Coursera, YouTube, etc.).
- The digitalization of businesses and processes results in basically every action made by individuals becoming traceable, measurable, and available for business decision-making.

© Springer Fachmedien Wiesbaden GmbH, part of Springer Nature 2021
C. Cramer, A. Thams, *Airline Revenue Management*,
https://doi.org/10.1007/978-3-658-33721-6_7

- Modern system architectures allow near-real-time processing of these actions on a global scale (with Hadoop and Spark as canonical examples).
- Infrastructures to host these system architectures and to store the data have become comparably cheap (in terms of unit cost) and instantly accessible by anyone through cloud platforms such as AWS, Azure, GCP, and DigitalOcean without the need for large initial capital outlays.

In this chapter, we aim at providing the reader with a structured overview of data science, specific techniques relevant to the field of revenue management, and practical aspects of technically and organizationally implementing data science applications.

7.1 The Fundamental Idea(s) Behind Data Science

There are many different definitions and interpretations of the topic "data science" which acts as an umbrella term for a certain set of capabilities, skillsets, and approaches. This often leads to misaligned expectations, even within a single organization, and perceptions of skill gaps or of labor market shortages, etc. For the purpose of this book and also in our professional experience, data science consists of *model-based analytical approaches* to solving business problems.

7.1.1 Understanding Analytics: Model-based Analytical Approaches

Several frameworks for understanding or defining model-based approaches exist, one typical example is shown below (Fig. 7.1):

A comprehensive overview of these frameworks is given in Vorhölter K., Greefrath G., Borromeo Ferri R., Leiß D., Schukajlow S. (2019) Mathematical Modelling. In: Jahnke H., Hefendehl-Hebeker L. (eds) Traditions in German-Speaking Mathematics Education Research. ICME-13 Monographs. Springer, Cham. https://doi.org/10.1007/978-3-030-11069-7_4.

For our purposes, an analytical model and the application of a model-based approach at the minimum consist of:

- *Real-world object*: The business entity or process we are ultimately interested in for the purpose of improving/optimizing certain aspects about it, e.g., this can be an aircraft with its seats or the airline booking process.
- *Model*: A model is a simplified abstraction of the real-world object. It is simplified in the sense that it only captures those aspects of the real-world object that are necessary for achieving the intended outcome (improvement/optimization). The simplification also implies that the included aspects do not necessarily need to achieve 100% fidelity, but can have an allowed degree of error which is explicitly or implicitly defined by the intended outcome.

7.1 The Fundamental Idea(s) Behind Data Science

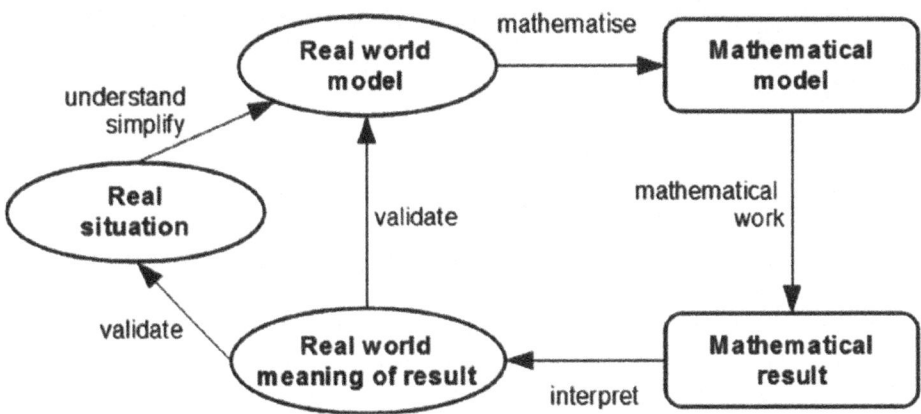

Fig. 7.1 Conceptual diagram of a mathematical model of a real situation (see Kaiser, G., & Stender, P. (2013). Complex modelling problems in co-operative, self-directed learning environments. In G. Stillman, G. Kaiser, W. Blum, & J. Brown (Eds.), *Teaching mathematical modelling: Connecting to research and practice* (pp. 277–293). Dordrecht: Springer)

For example, to model an aircraft for understanding its utilization, we do not need to know the size of a seat or its engine configuration, we simply need to know how many seats there are for each booking class. Likewise, for understanding booking curves, we do not need to know the gender or place of residence of customers, but it is helpful to know whether a customer is looking for a flight for personal or business purposes.

- *Observations*: These are recordings/measurements of the object's behavior or state. We use these observations to adjust and tune our model's behavior to be in line with the real-world object, i.e., to reduce/minimize the error between observations from the model and comparable observations from the real-world object, e.g., through the booking systems, we can observe which seats of an aircraft are booked at any given time and we can also observe when those bookings are made for which specific flight.
- *Inference*: What we are ultimately interested in is to use the model in order to understand and improve/optimize our real-world object by e.g., querying, manipulating, simulating situations/scenarios *which we have not observed in the past* and/or *for which it would be too costly or impossible to re-enact the situation in the real world*. For example, if we are to get an understanding of the booking behavior for a new leg in an airline's flight network, we have to develop a model for it simply because the leg does not exist yet.

Inference can either be used as a decision-support tool (humans interpreting model results and making decision based on them) or as automated decision tools (model results being used for decision automation, e.g., as in dynamic pricing).

Note that historically, decision-making in businesses is based on *mental models*. That is, managers observe their business by reading financial and operational KPI reports, talking to colleagues and employees or customers. They have a mental model of their business that is shaped by their prior experience and calibrated by their interpretation of which actions led to which changes. It is based on these mental models how they ultimately make decisions.

While successful and necessary in many areas and ways, however, this decision-making style is in fact limited by the human element:

- We cannot factor in all available data about the real-world object or about related objects since our mental capacity is limited in size and speed.
- We are not able to decide individually for several hundreds, thousands, not to mention millions of objects at the same time (e.g., which customer to target with which offer).
- We cannot simply transfer and scale the decision-making ability to other persons, e.g., newly hired employees. It takes a long time to do so through training, learning, etc., and will inevitably result in individual and therefore inconsistent decision styles.
- Lastly, we are humans with human interests and errors that will more or less interfere with the goal of optimal decisions from the business perspective.

Analytical models are ideally suited for scaling optimal decision-making to a fine-grained level of real-world business objects (e.g., customers, aircraft seats). The business discipline of airline revenue management is a prime example of an application area of model-based analytical approaches. Considering the value streams of an airline, we broadly seek to improve two main levers:

1. We want to maximize turnover by optimizing the combination of price per seat and utilization of seats, which are perishable assets.
2. We want to maximize turnover from ancillary sales, i.e., maximize customer value for a purchased flight along the whole journey from flight booking through to arrival at the destination.

There is a whole range of aspects connected to these two levers that can be described through analytical models, e.g.:

- Segmenting customers by their needs and their willingness to pay in order to differentiate and define booking classes
- Forecasting the demand for each booking class
- Maximizing the profit within each booking class using price/demand curves
- Targeting customers with offers for ancillary sales

7.1.2 Applying Analytics: A Taxonomy of Modern Analytical Methods

In the first part of the book, the reader has received an in-depth introduction into revenue management applications and the classical analytical methods employed for them, i.e., EM and statistical forecasting (moving averages, ARMA, exponential smoothing).

7.1 The Fundamental Idea(s) Behind Data Science

The modern analytical toolkit (in the practical scope defined by us) builds upon these methods and overall consists of three branches which we are going to describe in the remainder of this section:

- Statistics
- Mathematical optimization (operations research)
- Machine learning

7.1.2.1 Statistics

Statistics and *statistical modeling* help answering questions like "Given x, how likely is y?", alternatively formulated as "What is most likely given x?". To do so, statistics heavily draws on the concept of probability distributions to enable inference and testing. Probability describes the certainty or relative occurrence of events happening, usually in the form of mathematical formulas.

Many natural phenomena follow well-known probability distributions or can be described in the form of probability distributions. For example, the time between two customers arriving in a queue (or booking channel) or the number of customers who so far arrived in a queue follow the exponential and the Poisson distribution, respectively.

Probability distributions are general functions that become specific to the modeled problem by adjusting their *parameters*. We can determine the parameters by estimating them from observing a number of the associated events (a so-called sample).

Now, statistical theory enables us to make judgments about the *error* associated with these parameter estimates: e.g., if we have observed ten customers and the observed average time between their arrivals was twelve minutes, what is the most likely time between the arrivals of any of our future customers? How many customers do we have to observe to make a sound judgment? Do we have the same arrival behavior at queue A vs. queue B? Is the difference between arrival times at queue A vs. queue B a real difference or did we just observe a difference by chance because we looked at too few customers (i.e., was our sample size too small)?

In our view, the importance of statistics often gets overlooked with the hype around machine learning for two reasons:

1. The modeling step as such: It is vital to understand the statistical properties of process being model and of the data generation from the process. If our data sets are too small, we are essentially modeling chance occurrences that do not represent real-world situations.
2. The application of models: If we are to understand whether our models result in the effects intended for the modeled process, we have to measure and compare the process results against their pre-model-application state. Also, we have to measure and compare the underlying data properties against the state they were in when we were developing the model. If the model does not result in measurable improvements, we should not

make the effort to keep it running. If the properties of the process change, we have to adjust the machine learning model.

7.1.2.2 Mathematical Optimization

Mathematical optimization helps solving problems like "Given x, find *the best* y." (or alternatively formulated as: "Given x, find variable values z to get the best y."). This type of problem is specified by three components:

1. The *objective function*: The function whose value is to be minimized or maximized.
2. *Constraints*: Conditions that need to be fulfilled for a solution to be feasible—can, e.g., be ranges for the decision variables or joint conditions on several decision variables (e.g., if one variable needs to always be smaller than another)
3. *Decision variables*: The parameters that can be modified. Possible solutions to the problem are comprised of specific values for all parameters.

To paraphrase, in a mathematical optimization problem, our goal is to *maximize the objective function by varying the decision variables with a given set of constraints*. More intuitively, we can describe this concept as follows: The decision variables span the search space in which the optimal target (i.e., the solution to our problem) is to be found. The constraints limit the search space for the solution—mathematically speaking, the constrained decision variables form the objective function's domain. Lastly, the objective function creates a "shape" (graphically speaking, with mountains, saddles, and valleys) over its domain and we need to find the shape's extreme points by means of an optimization algorithm that efficiently walks through the search space.

The efficiency of finding a solution or respectively, the hardness of the optimization problem or of finding the extreme points depends on the structural properties of the constraints and of the objective function. Solutions for linear problems where we essentially look at the intersections planes can be easily found. Combinatorial optimization where essentially all possible solutions need to be enumerated and evaluated is hard, especially when dealing with non-convex problems where the shape of the objective function is not "mountainous" with clear directions to search in.

Optimization problems have characteristics that distinguish them from other data science problems; the methodology is specialized in that a problem cannot be either solved through optimization or by machine learning, but there specific problems that can be solved through optimization problems alone. Also, we often observed combined methodological approaches in practice where, e.g., a forecast is generated through statistical or machine learning methodologies, and decisions based on this forecast are made with an optimization model—such as the definition of overbooking limits.

The specific characteristics of optimization problems are as follows:

- The objective function needs to be described in *algebraic form*, i.e., there needs to be a very concrete and detailed understanding of cause-effect relationships for the problem.

7.1 The Fundamental Idea(s) Behind Data Science

- All decision variables need to be known and described.
- In general, formulating problems as optimization problems requires a deep understanding of the problem to be solved and a high degree of mathematical formalism.

Mathematical optimization is one of the disciplines in the field of *operations research* that covers applied mathematical approaches for many relevant business functions such as supply chain management and sales/customer service. We highly recommend to not overlook this field despite its perceived age and maturity and the relative skill shortage compared to an abundance of machine learning data scientists.

7.1.2.3 Machine Learning

Broadly speaking, *machine learning* can help with classification ("Is this an A or a B?") and regression (determining a numerical value for a set of inputs) tasks. Machine learning algorithms can be seen as generalized function approximators. They are shown a number of training examples ("this is an A," "this is a B") from which they parametrize a general function to become specific enough to closely reproduce ("learn") the training examples while also being able to generalize on unseen examples.

The power of machine learning algorithms stems from their practical relevance: There are several algorithms that are capable of generalizing over a broad range of different business problems. Also, in many cases, the data scientist does not need to dive deep into the mechanics of the various algorithms but can work with simple-to-use software packages. In practice, care has to be taken not to be deceived by the apparent ease of use and simplicity, since the majority fraction of work is concerned with understanding the statistical properties of the underlying training examples, appropriately formulating the inputs to the machine learning algorithm, and correctly evaluating and interpreting the machine learning model results.

With machine learning research dating back into the 1960s and significant advancements in the recent past, many methods applicable to different problems are available "off the shelf". Typical models encountered in practice are linear regression, gradient boosting, support vector machines, and various types of neural networks. These models typically are very good at dealing with high-dimensional problems (many input parameters), yet also are quite simple in what they produce, i.e., they predict values or points. They usually have an underlying assumption of the data and error distribution, but as a result of the way they are constructed, they do not allow easy statistical inference on their result. Machine learning models typically do not produce probability distributions of their predictions which, however, is quite relevant for business problems, e.g., we are usually not only interested in how many passengers we expect to book a certain flight on a given date, but also in the probability of different outcomes.

Current research (Bayesian machine learning, probabilistic machine learning) is advancing the state of the art for these business questions and an important development to look out for. Another research area that has resulted in significant practical advances is that of representation learning (e.g., embeddings and autoencoders) where high-dimensional data is (implicitly) reduced to lower-dimensional representations which are not only compressed but also convey additional meaning in the data, describing similarities. Machine learning methods for text and image data have demonstrated the large performance increases possible from leveraging these encoding techniques and other high-dimensional data like e-commerce clickstreams, purchases, and customer profiles also stand to benefit from their application.

In summary, statistics, mathematical optimization, and machine learning are three quite distinct disciplines that are not necessarily interchangeable when solving problems, but in our experience, they are valuable complements. When building a commercial data science capability, we caution the reader to not have a single-minded focus on machine learning skills, but to create a balanced skillset mix out of the described disciplines.

7.1.3 The Analytical Cycle: Solving Business Problems with Analytical Methods

Having described the background and core disciplines of data science, we now provide the reader with practical insights into successfully executing data science projects. A good mental model for structuring this kind of project is the "Cross-Industry Standard Process for Data Mining" or CRISP-DM as depicted below. Note that we do not necessarily recommend to set up strict project frameworks with checklists, gates, etc. as this depends on the culture and context of the reader's respective business. However, we want to highlight the key points to know and consider in a data science project when compared to other projects, be it business or IT projects. For any other details of the process, we refer the reader to a vast body of standard literature on the subject, the Wikipedia page provides a set of references (https://en.wikipedia.org/wiki/Cross-industry_standard_process_for_data_mining) (Fig. 7.2).

Those key points are:

- It is not a coincidence that the process starts with the phase of *business understanding*. Data scientists, especially those from a purely technical or scientific background, often have the urge to start diving into data, developing interesting model architectures, and tuning model performance to a high level. However, it is absolutely paramount to first understand what the actual business problem is that needs to be solved. This involves talking to the business stakeholders, questioning them about their current pain points and how exactly a good solution or result should look like. In this phase, we highly recommend to spend time with the users of an application that needs to be improved or the actors in a process that needs to be optimized/automated. Understanding their point of view is often crucial in defining the right modeling approach as well as determining the target that needs to be achieved—and to what degree.
- Closely linked to the first phase—and therefore also described as a cycle in the model— is the next phase of *data understanding*. Again, data scientists tend to see this phase or activity as a rather mechanical task to look at distributions, missing values, value

7.1 The Fundamental Idea(s) Behind Data Science

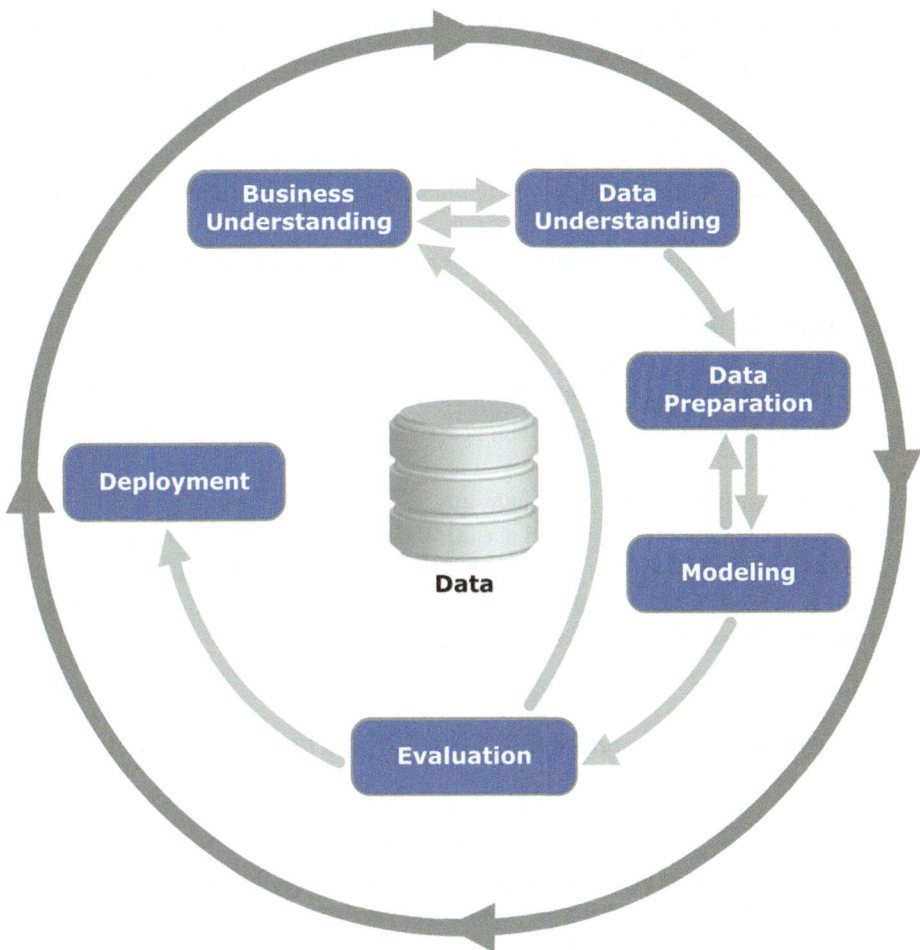

Fig. 7.2 CRISP-DM, the cross-industry standard process for data mining (this depiction (C) Kenneth Jensen)

encodings, etc. It is, however, even more important to understand how the *data-generating process* looked or looks like. That is, which parts of the underlying business process were measured and how? Are there circumstances under which relevant data is not or not uniquely recorded? Has the data only been recorded at certain points in time? Do we need to measure and record additional data in order to come up with good modeling and solution approach?

- The choice of models should predominantly be guided by practicality reasons. More complicated models are likely to be more "brittle" to maintain, also in many cases, the financial cost of (re-)training them can significantly reduce their business benefit. For example, we have seen several cases where neural-network-based forecasting models

have been discarded in favor of computationally more simple gradient boosting models since these had a much lower unit operating cost (because they do not require more expensive GPU computation).
- The evaluation of a model should not solely be based on mathematical error metrics focusing on the mechanics on the model. There needs to be a clear definition of the business value generated by the model improvement, e.g., additional revenue or reduced cost.
- Lastly, a data science project is not finished when a good model has been developed, but this model needs to meet reality by being integrated into business applications or by developing new decision tools. The models themselves also have a lifecycle since their performance or the underlying business process data can change over time. There needs to be a responsibility to monitor the performance in production and to adjust or ultimately decommission a model when necessary.

As can be seen from the iterative nature of the cycle itself, the milestones for a data science project cannot be fully planned ahead. We recommend to rather understand time planning for this kind of project as time-boxing where time is allotted to the different phases in order to avoid, e.g., overly detailed modeling. Business environments that favor agile project are most suitable for data science projects.

7.2 Engineering Analytics: Big Data Infrastructure and Data Pipelines

Some years before the current interest in data science, "big data" was coined as a term for the vast amounts of data getting created and becoming more and more accessible by businesses. The McKinsey & Company report "Big data: The next frontier" (2011) helped popularize the term. In the context of analytics and data science applications, we understand "big data" as the underlying *database technologies*, not as an artificial definition of data set sizes.

Traditionally, applications store their data in relational databases (e.g., PostgreSQL, MySQL, SQL Server, DB2, Oracle) and data gets consolidated into data warehouses (e.g., Teradata, SAP BW) for analytical purposes. Their system architectures have in common that they have been designed for data center environments in which the only way to deal with increasing system load was to increase the capacity (CPU cores and speed, RAM, disk) of the server hosting the system, that is by "scaling up" (vertically).

Because of the physical limits of scaling up, Internet companies designed data systems that are able to scale horizontally ("scaling out"). In these system architectures, data storage and processing get automatically distributed across multiple servers in a data center. Yahoo and Google have pioneered the development with Hadoop and MapReduce being key early big data technologies.

In contrast to traditional database technologies, their explicit goal is not to act as an operational data store for application systems and therefore do not guarantee transactional safety or high-speed/high-volume data inserts. Their goal is to enable high-volume data queries that can scale virtually limitless.

One of their properties is, however, that they only operate on *batch* workloads. That is, they are not designed to support interactive queries or even (near) real-time queries on the data store for operational applications. Their purpose is to support analytical workloads where delays of several hours between sending a query and getting a result are allowed to pass. These workloads can either be initiated by analysts or by applications that, e.g., perform daily recalculations of queries.

To address the need for more interactive or less delay-tolerant workloads, the so-called *lambda architecture* has been designed to add a *streaming layer* to batch-oriented data stores. The streaming layer enables fast access to, e.g., the most recent data in a system. An example technology commonly used for the streaming layer is Apache Spark.

However, in any case, the addition of batching and streaming layers to database and data warehouse systems only considers analytical and other data applications as an afterthought. With each intermediate step in such a data pipeline, the risk of decreasing data accuracy as well as the delay from data origination to data use increases. Even more recent systems are built around the abstraction of a log ("*log-structured systems*") (Fig. 7.3).

Here, applications stream their data into a log which ultimately is enabled by a distributed system. The log provides a publish-subscribe abstraction where a downstream system can subscribe to the application events and, e.g., persist the most recent event in a database, perform aggregations in a data warehouse, or derive predictions based on the event. This abstraction mitigates the above-mentioned risks.

In our experience, considering a data warehouse as a data source for data science applications should only serve as a stop-gap solution while implementing more direct data pipelines through log-structured abstractions. The closer the data science application needs to be to the source in terms of speed and quality, the more problematic traditional data warehouses become.

A prime example of log-structured systems is Apache Kafka. Delta Lake by Databricks offers a more database-like experience where both access to real-time streams and to persisted intermediate event status is provided.

We refer the interested reader to the excellent resource Designing Data-Intensive Applications by Martin Kleppmann (2017) for an in-depth look into the evolution of data system architectures and for practical advice on data pipeline construction.

7.3 Managing Analytics: Structuring Analytical Capabilities and Processes

Having understood the purpose and the basics of data science, the most important question remaining from a business perspective is how to manage such a capability within a company. When discussing this with top managers in less experienced companies, you often hear questions like "Do we hire a few data scientists and put them into IT?" "We

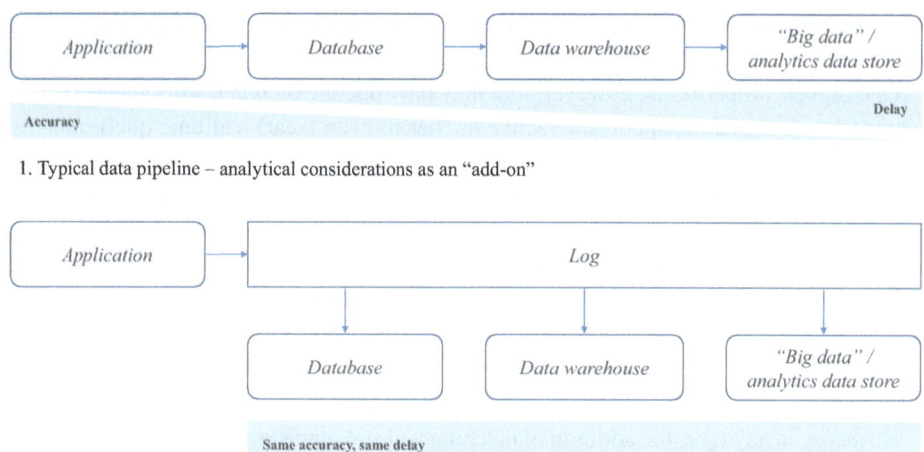

Fig. 7.3 Structure of data pipelines

already have digital marketing analysts, can they go on to roll out data science in our company?" "What do we need to look for when hiring?" or "Do we need to hire 100 data scientists and spread them across the company?".

In its essence, it comes down to where and how to get started. We would like to provide the reader with a few practical guidelines and experiences; however, those strongly depend on the reader's respective context and on the respective level of maturity of the topic in the company.

1. *Data science is a business capability*: Like any other technology, data science is a means to an end. We have seen many cases where—because of the perceived closeness to technology-related issues such as cloud computing—data science capabilities were placed into IT functions. Sadly, if the IT function in your company is not being perceived and accepted as a partner in helping business evolve, the data science capability also will not have the right leverage. We recommend placing the capability into a strategic function in the business that closely works with other business functions or divisions in order to help them solve their problems.
2. *Data science is not business intelligence (BI)*: BI often is a well-established function that is not seen as too innovative, as well as being limited by a long pipeline of requests for creating new reports. There is a considerable risk that data science gets perceived in the same way if you integrate both capabilities in one function. Furthermore, you will want to have a clear skillset separation in order to avoid your data scientists working on BI reports and data visualizations. However, there are strong synergies between the two capabilities since data science work often requires good and intuitive visualization of model results.

7.3 Managing Analytics: Structuring Analytical Capabilities and Processes

3. *Do not focus on "machine learning nerds" in your hiring strategy*: To successfully establish a data science capability that closely works with business functions on their problems, you need persons who understand how a business works, how projects are implemented in a business, and how to deliver results from data science methodologies. Unless you are in the business of building machine learning platforms or services, you will generate less traction or in the worst case, a clear divide between business and data science functions if you focus on hiring technical experts that only know the bleeding edge of machine learning research, but cannot relate to business stakeholders and their problems. Think of the data science capability as an internal consultancy that needs to deliver projects with a special skill set. Build your team from that idea.

4. *Data science is a scarce resource*: This is especially true if you start building the capability "from scratch" within your company. If you immediately place large numbers of data scientists into various parts of the business, you will have a hard time creating a shared vision, strategy, and effective process for both the data science teams, but also for all business areas working with the data scientists. We, therefore, recommend to start small and with a centralized team. The technical/methodological skills can be more general in the beginning in order to be able to serve different parts of the business at the same time. Leverage these resources to generate the most value, i.e., allocate them to the most valuable projects that also quickly generate results and interest in the capability. Scale the team up together with project demand across the company. It will quickly become apparent which business areas already are or can become mature enough to "host" their own and potentially specialized data science capabilities (e.g., by function such as logistics, marketing, sales, or by division), which marks the start of a successive decentralization. We are strongly convinced that over time, data science needs to be an embedded capability in any (relevant) part of a company. However, we also recommend to retain a centralized core capability that stays responsible for advancing the data science operations processes, for investigating state-of-the-art methodologies, and for driving explorative and innovative projects.

Since we argued that a data science function should be situated in the business and since data science clearly has a close proximity to technology, another aspect to consider is the split of responsibilities with IT. Again, we will provide the reader with viewpoints and insights derived from our practical experience, but note that this is an area evolving with the technology itself and therefore boundaries are shifting quite rapidly. Interested readers should keep an eye on new developments in DevOps, Kubernetes in relation to data science applications, and especially MLOps.

1. *IT as a platform provider*: Ideally, your IT function provides all necessary infrastructures and platforms to enable your data science teams to independently work along the whole lifecycle of your data science projects. The platforms, therefore, need to include database systems for data sourcing, data processing tools (e.g., Spark), and app deployment platforms (e.g., Docker/Kubernetes). To adhere to general IT standards,

however, the data science teams will have to adopt shared best practices with regard to versioning, coding, etc. early on. On the other hand, we have seen many cases where there was a clear split between data science and IT teams along the lifecycle stages of a project without common platforms; this inevitably leads to rework by re-platforming, recoding, redesign of models and therefore increases the lead time to results for the business functions supposed to benefit from the projects.

2. *Analytical applications are not your typical IT applications*: While these applications behave like normal IT applications and need to be managed according to standard maintenance and service practices, it is crucial to understand that the *analytical models integrated* into those applications require a different type of monitoring and maintenance as well. Since business realities do not stop with the initial development completion of a model, we can observe two effects in practice: that of *data drift* (the underlying statistics of the process modeled shift, e.g., from changing customer demand, competition, etc.) and that of *model drift* (the predictive quality of a model may worsen over time if left unattended). These two effects need to be specifically monitored and cared for along with the regular application and platform monitoring. However, this specific monitoring task ought to be performed by the data science capability since it is focusing on non-technical performance KPIs directly related to business performance. This is not a task that can simply be handed over to IT, but data science team members need to be involved when certain limits in data and/or model drift are exceeded to take appropriate action. Note that this follows the same analytical cycle we outlined before.

3. *Data science needs an operations team with (some) IT skills:* In the mental model of many top managers, data science team members continuously churn out new analytical products and applications and do nothing else. However, if your ambition is not to only produce PowerPoint reports based on data science results, but create real business leverage from incorporating models into processes and applications, as outlined above, these models will require a constant maintenance effort by the data science team. Also, the data scientists will continue to improve and change the analytical applications based on the business needs. There are two points that we would like to explicitly highlight in this: first, this means that your data science team will need a scale for those tasks over time and needs to be understood by and made transparent for the business sponsors of the data science capability. Second, by nature of these tasks, they are close to IT operations tasks and will inevitably cause discussions about responsibilities of business vs. IT departments in typical organizations. It, therefore, is important to have early and up-front alignments with IT stakeholders on a joint operating model for data science applications.

7.4 Data Science—Revenue Management Use Cases

In the remaining part of this chapter, we will demonstrate how data science and the data science process discussed before play a practical role in revenue management.

7.4 Data Science—Revenue Management Use Cases

The goal is to show the reader how the process looks like in concrete business-related examples. We provide a worked example that includes code examples for illustration purposes; they are not intended to be detailed programming examples, but rather to show how thinking in the process and working with data often looks like.

For readers who would like to continue their data science journey, we provide a detailed bibliography at the end of the chapter.

We have chosen a use case that specifically underlines our previous argument that data science does not consist of a single type of methodology, but that solving each business problem/use case may require methodologies from different branches of mathematics or computer science.

7.4.1 Data Science—Use Case: Mid-/long-term Demand Forecasting

7.4.1.1 Business Problem

Consider an airline that at the beginning of a business year needs to create (update) an 18-month demand forecast in order to provide input to the operational planning processes to ultimately budget for the resources (e.g., flight capacities (planes), slots and ground operations, crew resources, etc.) that will be needed to meet the demand.

For this use case:

- Demand is defined as the number of passengers.
- The forecasting horizon is 18 months and demand is to be forecast on a monthly level.
- The number of passengers needs to be forecast for each one-way flight leg.
- The forecast needs to be a point forecast that is as precise as possible (i.e., we need to forecast a concrete number of passengers, not a range, and in the evaluation, no difference is being made between over- vs. underforecasting the actual number of passengers).
- We are using the domestic route FRA-MUC in Germany as our specific forecasting case.

7.4.1.2 Data Sourcing and Structure

The airline would create an unconstrained (market view) and a constrained (airline view) demand forecast. Here, we are going to focus on the unconstrained demand forecast for data availability reasons; the constrained demand forecast is created with the same methodology, but based on internal data sources (e.g., CRS, controlling systems).

Detailed statistics about domestic and international flights originating or landing in Germany are gathered by the Federal Statistical Office of Germany and published on a monthly basis. Unfortunately, these statistics cannot be queried from a database, but are provided in the form of Excel spreadsheets. This is quite a typical situation in many data science projects, also for company-internal data sources.

Data is taken from the publication *Gewerblicher Luftverkehr (monatlich), Sachtitel: Fachserie. 8, Verkehr. 6, Luftverkehr*. There are over 200 spreadsheets dating back to the year 2002. Each monthly publication is a sub-webpage linked to from the main site of the publication series. The key challenges are that:

- There are too many files to download manually since it is time-consuming and error-prone, therefore we need to automatically download them.
- The links to the spreadsheets on the sub-pages are not part of the HTML document but are dynamically generated through JavaScript, therefore we need to create custom code to extract document and identifiers and reconstruct download links.
- Over such a long time span, the document format does not stay the same.

We retrieved all of the spreadsheets by using the very good and versatile web scraping library called *scrapy*. The crawler consists of only three short functions, (1) parse which extracts all links to the document sub-pages from the publication's main site, (2) parse_monthly which generates the download links on each sub-page, and (3) save_file to download the documents themselves.

```
import scrapy
from scrapy.http.request import Request

class DestatisSpider(scrapy.Spider):
    name = 'destatis'
    start_urls =
['https://www.statistischebibliothek.de/mir/receive/
    DESerie_mods_00000093']

    def parse(self, response):
        doc_links =
response.css('.detail_block').xpath('./ul/li/a/@href').getall()
        yield from response.follow_all(doc_links, self.parse_monthly)

    def parse_monthly(self, response):
        data_deriID = response.css('.file_box_files').xpath('./
@data-deriid').getall()
        data_mainDoc = response.css('.file_box_files').xpath('./
@data-maindoc').getall()

        file_urls = ["{}/{}/{}".format("https://www.
statistischebibliothek.de/mir/servlets/MCRFileNodeServlet", a, b)
for a,b in zip(data_deriID, data_mainDoc)]

        for url in file_urls:
            yield Request(url, callback=self.save_file)
```

(continued)

7.4 Data Science—Revenue Management Use Cases

```
def save_file(self, response):
    path = response.url.split('/')[-1]
    with open(path, "wb") as f:
        f.write(response.body)
```

For the next step, extracting the data from the downloaded Excel spreadsheets, we used the Python library openpyxl which can only access the ".xslx" format, not the older ".xls" format. In our case, we used Automator on Mac OS X to convert all files as required (Fig. 7.4).

Being able to automate parts of your data science process comes in handy; it does not have to be implemented in the same language as the mathematical models, shell programming and other operating system tools often are good choices.

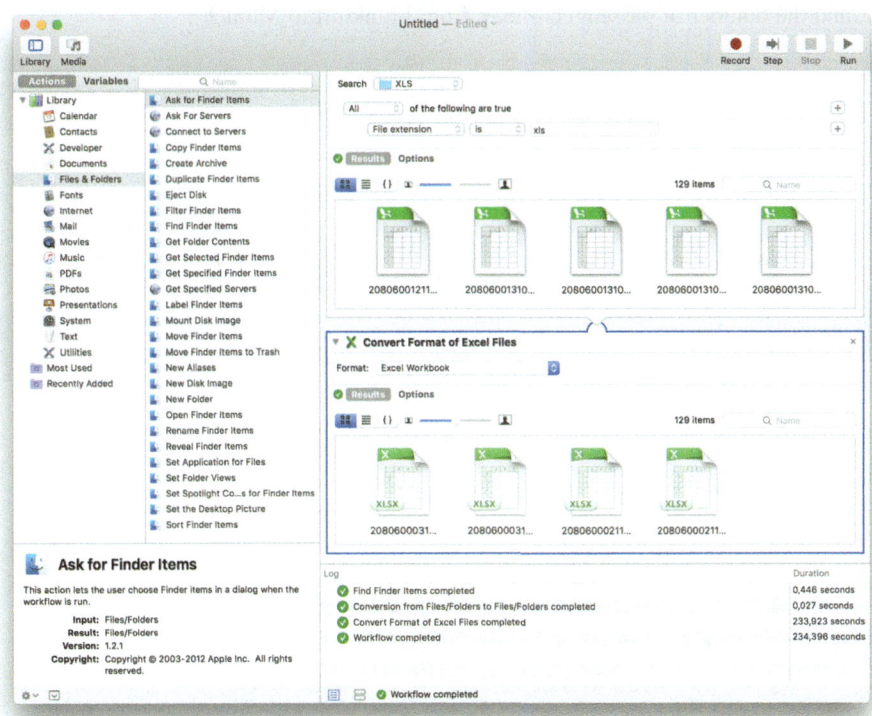

Fig. 7.4 Conversion of xls to xlsx format prior to openpyxl import

The structure of the spreadsheets is most consistent over the years: there is a title page containing the month and year, and the individual sheets containing the data have the same names as well as columns/table headings. However, there is a change in the reporting logic from 2010 to 2011 which also results in different passenger numbers. We therefore only regarded data starting in 2011, but this also more than sufficient. For our forecasting purpose, it is necessary to have at least three years of data:

- The first year to learn patterns from (train set)
- The second year to evaluate and tune the predictive power of our forecasting model (validation set)
- The third year to finally evaluate the predictive power after tuning in a blind test (holdout or test set)

In order to extract the data from the downloaded spreadsheets, we iterate over them and then search for the source/destination airport combination in the worksheet containing domestic passengers flown from source to destination, and finally output file name, period date, and the number of passengers (here: from Frankfurt to Munich):

```
try:
    ws = wb['1.3.2']
except KeyError:
    continue

src = 'Frankfurt'
src_cell = None
dst = 'München'
dst_cell = None

for row in ws.iter_rows(min_col=1, max_col=1):
    for cell in takewhile(lambda x: dst_cell == None, row):
        val = str(cell.value).lstrip()
        if val.startswith(src):
            src_cell = cell
            adj_cell = src_cell.offset(0,1)
            val_adj = str(adj_cell.value).lstrip()
            if val_adj.startswith(dst):
                dst_cell = adj_cell

col_idx = dst_cell.col_idx + 3
row_idx = src_cell.row

pax = ws.cell(row=row_idx, column=col_idx).value

print("{},{},{}".format(name, date, pax))
```

7.4 Data Science—Revenue Management Use Cases

As a result, we have the raw data in a CSV structure that we can process for our forecasts in one of the next steps.

7.4.1.3 Methodological Problem

Before starting with the development of the actual modeling/forecasting approach, we take a look at the data to 1) get a first understanding of the structure of the business problem we are dealing with and 2) identify any potential issues with our data, i.e., errors or limitations.

Reading in the data we downloaded before is straightforward, we only have to ensure that the Pandas data frame gets a time series index:

```
import pandas as pd
import matplotlib.pyplot as plt

demand_ts = pd.read_csv('/mnt/My Drive/destatis/fra_muc_v4.csv',
sep=';')
demand_ts = demand_ts.set_index(pd.to_datetime(demand_ts
[['year','month']].assign(day=1)))
```

A good way to understand the structure of the time series is to plot the time series itself as well its decomposition into trend, seasonal, and residual (= actual − trend − seasonal) components. "Seasonal and Trend decomposition using Loess" (STL) is a robust method to perform a first decomposition without making explicit model assumptions. Note that we defined a seasonal period of 13 months because from our knowledge about the business problem and by looking at the data, we know that there is an annual seasonality, and STL requires odd seasonalities (Fig. 7.5):

```
plt.rc('figure',figsize=(8,6))
plt.rc('font',size=13)

from statsmodels.tsa.seasonal import STL
stl = STL(demand_ts.pax, seasonal=13)
res = stl.fit()
fig = res.plot()
```

We can make some interesting observations from the decomposition:

- There is a very clear annual seasonality which only slightly changes over the 9-year period.
- The trend sees a stable, yet small increase over the same period—with an abrupt change c. around mid-/end 2019. Most of the change can be explained from the onset of the Covid-19 crisis at the beginning of 2020.

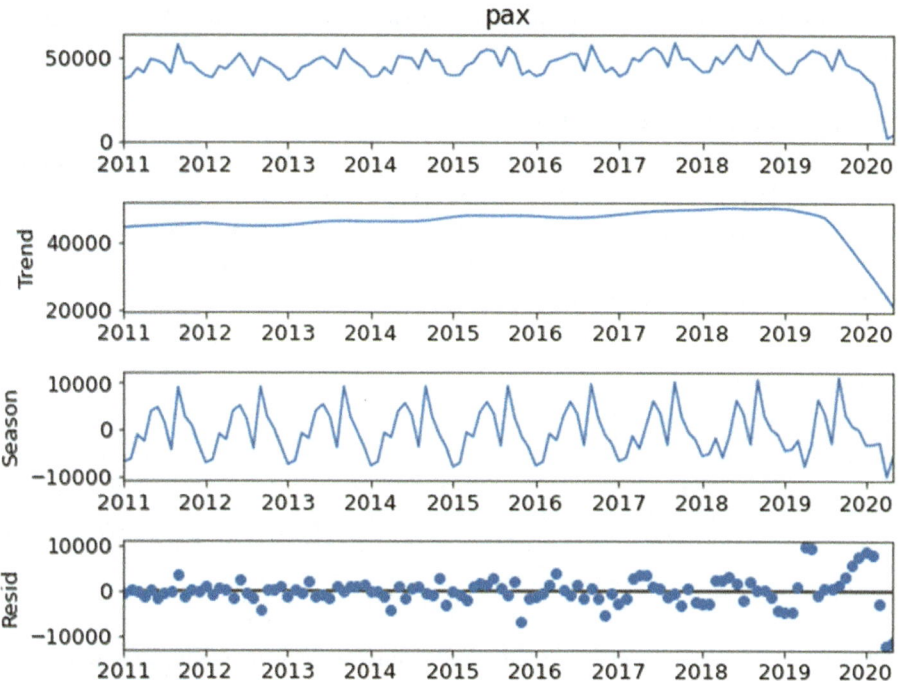

Fig. 7.5 STL decomposition of the PAX FRA-MUC traveled time series

- Also, the residuals seem to be randomly distributed without clear structural patterns—the last 2–3 years show hints of structural patterns which we would need to investigate for model making, e.g., normality assumptions. Especially the last year with the changing trend shows a clear structural pattern, violating such an assumption.

Since we cannot possibly forecast the COVID-19 effect and would therefore significantly alter our ability to forecast in our example case, we are removing all 2020 data from the data set (demand_ts = demand_ts.loc[:'2019-12-31']).

As we have several years of historical data, we can easily split it into training and validation sets. However, special care has to be taken when dealing with time series data. Unlike for general machine learning cases, we cannot draw randomized samples for the data set to create the split sets, but we have to preserve temporal structure, both within training and validation sets, but also across those sets: We must ensure that we do not create so-called *data leaks* where the training data references future points in time which could not have been known while the training data had been created. Therefore, training/validation sets need to be non-overlapping and sequentially ordered according to the individual data point's time stamps.

Also, since we want to predict 18 months into the future, it would be a waste of data if we would take all data points except for the last 18 to predict and then evaluate the

7.4 Data Science—Revenue Management Use Cases

comparison. The result would be a single performance metric without any sense of variation. To overcome these limitations, we employ *time-series cross validation*. With this method, the original data set gets split into multiple training and validation sets (each called "fold") with the split point "sliding" forward in time until there is insufficient data to create another validation set. In our case, we create splits each June so that our last validation set can end in December 2019. Here, split_idxs denotes the array indices along with the data set is split into training and validation sets each. Folds are stored as dictionaries in the folds array where training and validation sets are addressable via keys. With this step, basic data preparation for our problem is finished.

```
split_idxs = []
folds = []

for i in range(len(demand_ts.index)):
    if demand_ts.index[i].month == 6 and i >= 17 and i <= (len(demand_ts.index)-18):
        split_idxs.append(i+1)

for i in split_idxs:
    fold_dict = { "train": demand_ts[:i].copy(), "val": demand_ts[i:i+18].copy() }
    folds.append(fold_dict)
```

7.4.1.4 Goal Definition

There are several ways of measuring the accuracy of forecasts, each with pros and cons. An important consideration to make in our view is how intuitive a chosen metric will be for business stakeholders involved in the use case. We, therefore, prefer not to use the root mean squared error (RMSE), but to measure accuracy as the mean average percentage error (MAPE) defined as follows:

```
import numpy as np

def mape(y, y_hat):
    return np.mean(np.abs((y-y_hat) / y))
```

Discussions of this and other metrics can be found in the forecasting literature. The target value to set for the MAPE depends on the problem and the forecast level—for our use case with stable seasonalities and a medium forecast level (one flight route), we are aiming for an accuracy of at least 5%.

For this and for any data science use case in general, it is important to have a baseline value of the target metric to compare against. The baseline can either be the approach (incl.

any knowledge-driven heuristics or procedures) currently being used in a business process or a comparably simple method. With the baseline metric available, we can derive the additional value generated by using more sophisticated methods.

In our use case example, we do not have a specific business practice to compare against, we, therefore, use simple forecasting methods to determine the reference values. These methods specifically are:

- Naïve forecast: In this most basic method, we simply repeat the last value known in the time series as our forecast for the next value. That is, if our last known training value is from July 2018, we repeat the same value as our forecast for August 2018, September 2018, and all further months in the validation set (Fig. 7.6).

- Seasonal naïve forecast: This method is an extension of the naïve forecast honoring the fact that there is a seasonally repeating pattern in the time series data. Still being a basic method, it simply repeats the last value known in the time series *from the previous season* as our forecast for the current season. That is, with an assumed seasonality of 12 months, we forecast the value of August 2017 for August 2018, September 2017 for September 2018, and so on (Fig. 7.7).

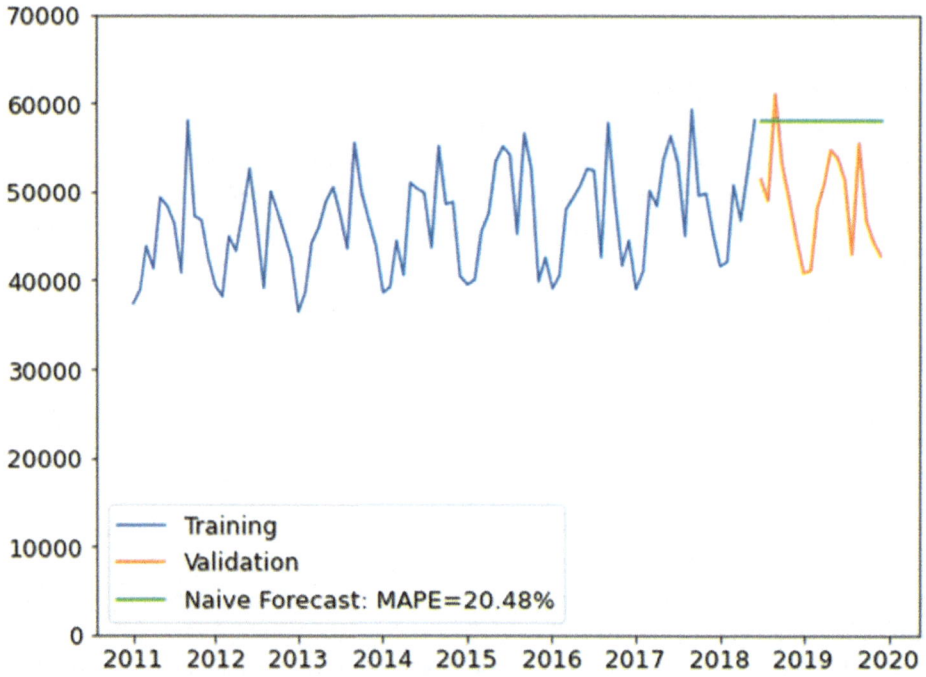

Fig. 7.6 Naïve forecast example

7.4 Data Science—Revenue Management Use Cases

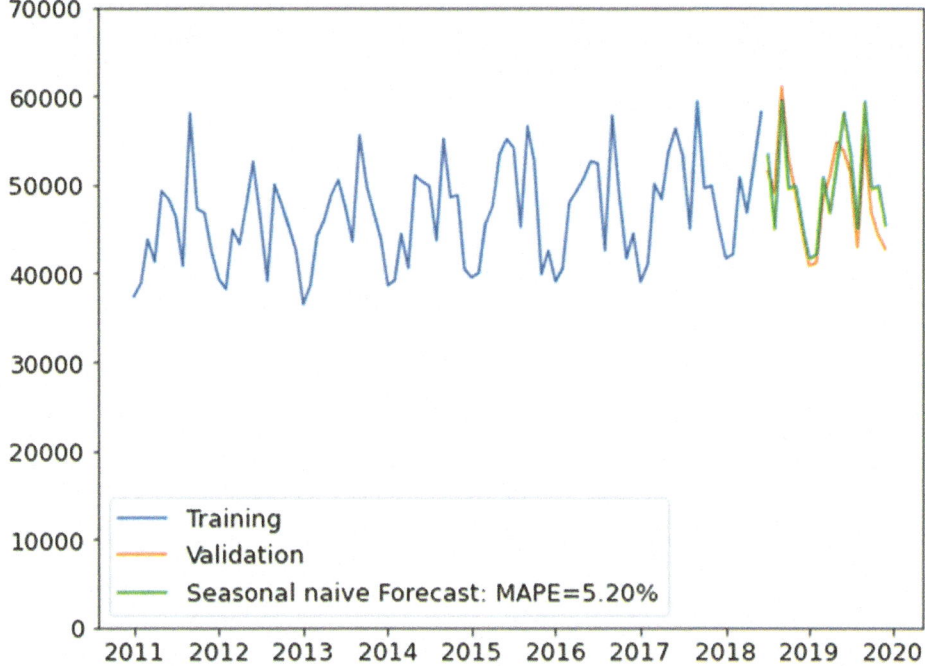

Fig. 7.7 Seasonal naïve forecast example

In the examples shown in both figures, we used August 2018–December 2019 as the forecasting and validation period (a so-called in-sample forecast since we are forecasting an already known period in the time series). Not unexpectedly, the naïve forecast results in an error (20.5%) that is quite far away from our self-defined target. The seasonal naïve forecast results in a much lower error (5.2%) which also already is close to our target.

However, both error values can also be random coincidences since we only looked at one validation period. This a practical example of why it is reasonable to have a solid understanding of statistics (and, e.g., not only machine learning) when approaching data science use cases: By systematically evaluating the forecasting error of both methods on multiple periods, we are able to extrapolate and judge their overall performance. The following code fragment evaluates both baseline forecasts for all training/validation folds (non-overlapping 18-month periods) and visualizes the forecast errors in the form of box plots:

```
mape_naive = []
mape_snaive = []

for f in folds:
    train = f["train"]
    val = f["val"]

    val.loc[:,'y_hat'] = train.pax[-1:].values
    val.loc[:,'y_hat_snaive'] = train.iloc[-12:].pax.values[[x %
12 for x in list(range(18))]]
    mape_naive.append(mape(val.pax, val.y_hat))
    mape_snaive.append(mape(val.pax, val.y_hat_snaive))

plt.figure(figsize=(8, 6))
plt.ylim(0.0,0.3)
plt.boxplot(mape_naive)

plt.figure(figsize=(8, 6))
plt.ylim(0.0,0.3)
plt.boxplot(mape_snaive)
```

The box plots summarize the distributional characteristics of the errors by highlighting the 25%/50% (median)/75% quantiles and the spread defined by the interquartile range (Figs. 7.8 and 7.9).

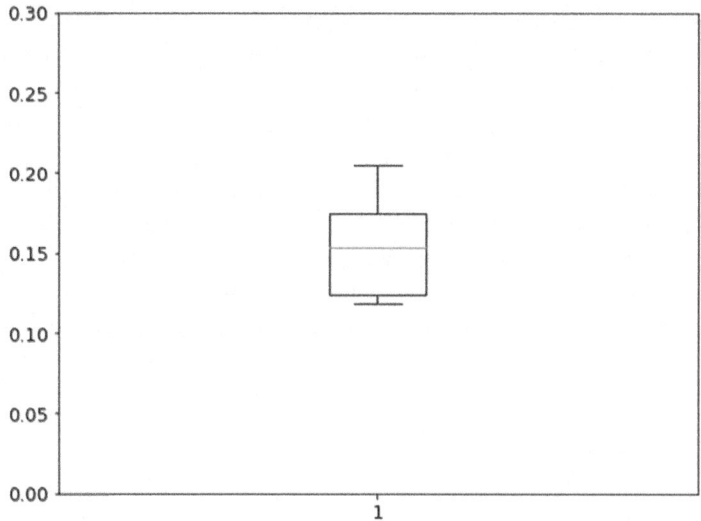

Fig. 7.8 Naive forecasting error (MAPE)

7.4 Data Science—Revenue Management Use Cases

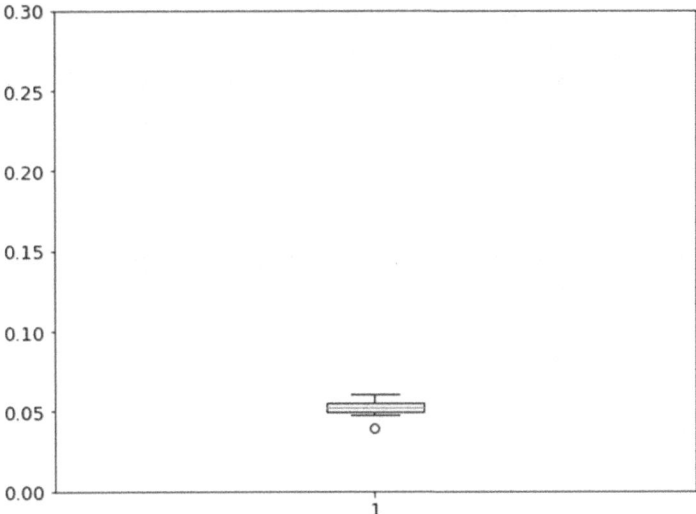

Fig. 7.9 Seasonal naive forecasting error (MAPE)

Again, we can see that the naïve forecast exhibits a consistently bad performance, but also that the 20.5% forecast error for the last forecasting period indeed was an extreme value when compared to the overall distribution. The seasonal naïve forecast exhibits a more stable performance with little variance over the different folds. Its median error is slightly above our target of 5% and hence, we will investigate how to improve this error by different methods in the remainder of this use case discussion.

7.4.1.5 Development of the Approach(es)

Having established the baseline to compare further methods against, we will now show the reader typical machine learning methods for time series forecasting and how to prepare the time series data for them. This section focuses on modeling and methodological aspects while the actual model results are compared in the next section.

In increasing order of intricacy, we will be constructing the following time series models:

- Linear regression with recursive feature elimination (RFE)
- An ensemble of the linear regression and seasonal naïve models
- Gradient boosting, i.e., XGBoost and LightGBM
- Long short-term memory (LSTM), i.e., a neural network

These models are regression models which can be interpreted as mathematical functions $y = f_\theta(x)$ where:

- y is forecast value (the number of passengers).
- x is a vector of features (historical values) used to calculate the forecast.

- f is the function class represented by the respective machine learning model (i.e., a linear equation for the linear regression model).
- θ is the set of parameters describing the specific instance of the function f; these parameters are generated by training the model, i.e., by minimizing the error between training examples and the forecast value of the parametrized function. For a linear regression model, θ is a matrix.

In order to formulate and train the model as such, we have to transform the time series data into appropriate feature vectors. Without transformation, our data is structured as follows:

```
train.iloc[-val.shape[0]:]
```

	orig_file	month	year	pax
2017-01-01	./destatis_v2/2080600171015.xlsx	1	2017	39042
2017-02-01	./destatis_v2/2080600171025.xlsx	2	2017	41093
2017-03-01	./destatis_v2/2080600171035.xlsx	3	2017	50139
2017-04-01	./destatis_v2/2080600171045.xlsx	4	2017	48414
2017-05-01	./destatis_v2/2080600171055.xlsx	5	2017	53687

Each table row corresponds to one data record or training example. In this structure, the examples only contain the historical number of passengers in a given month. Without further transformation, the models will not know how to relate different points in time to each other since they only consider one example at a time with no notion of time or sequence.

To pass this additional data to the models, we create so-called lagged features. That is, we expand each data record by the number of passengers in the month before (-1), two months before (-2), etc.:

7.4 Data Science—Revenue Management Use Cases

```
def create_features(y, input_lags=None):
    features = pd.DataFrame()

    if input_lags is None:
        lags = list(range(13))
        lags.remove(0)
    else:
        lags = input_lags

    for lag in lags:
        features["lag_{}".format(lag)] = y.shift(lag)

    features.index = y.index
    return (features, lags)

feat, lags = create_features(train.pax)
train = train[12:].merge(feat[12:], left_index=True,
right_index=True)
```

Besides the previous months' passenger number, we also know from our initial data exploration that there are strong seasonal patterns and therefore that there might be additional information derived from the month that we are forecasting itself. In the current structure of the data, months are encoded as integer numbers, but the models should not try to calculate passenger values based on the month's number. We, therefore, have to re-code the information by converting months into binary feature vectors:

```
train = pd.get_dummies(train, columns=['month'], drop_first=True,
prefix='month')
train.tail()
```

pax	lag_1	lag_2	lag_3	lag_4	lag_5	lag_6	lag_7	lag_8	lag_9	lag_10	lag_11	lag_12	month_2	month_3	month_4	month_5	mo
42140	41671.0	45452.0	49880.0	49590.0	59388.0	45039.0	53393.0	56376.0	53687.0	48414.0	50139.0	41093.0	1	0	0	0	
50853	42140.0	41671.0	45452.0	49880.0	49590.0	59388.0	45039.0	53393.0	56376.0	53687.0	48414.0	50139.0	0	1	0	0	
46790	50853.0	42140.0	41671.0	45452.0	49880.0	49590.0	59388.0	45039.0	53393.0	56376.0	53687.0	48414.0	0	0	1	0	
52323	46790.0	50853.0	42140.0	41671.0	45452.0	49880.0	49590.0	59388.0	45039.0	53393.0	56376.0	53687.0	0	0	0	1	
58180	52323.0	46790.0	50853.0	42140.0	41671.0	45452.0	49880.0	49590.0	59388.0	45039.0	53393.0	56376.0	0	0	0	0	

As the last step, we remove all unnecessary and unwanted data from the examples and structure it in the form of y, x (see above):

```
X=train.drop(['orig_file', 'year', 'pax'], axis=1)
y=train.pax
```

For the forecasting granularity needed for the use case discussed here, these likely already are enough features. If we would be looking at a higher-resolution forecasting granularity, for example, daily number of passengers, and with a larger and more varied scope, for example, routes from departure airports in all German states, the model could benefit from additional features such as the day of the week, whether there is a public holiday or not, etc.

Linear Regression with Recursive Feature Elimination (RFE)
Setting up and training the linear regression model now is straightforward:

```
from sklearn.linear_model import LinearRegression
from sklearn.feature_selection import RFE
model = LinearRegression()
lm = RFE(model, 8)

lm.fit(X,y)
```

In order to make forecasts on the validation set, we also have to create the necessary lagged features and month encodings. We can append the forecast next to the actual value in the validation set to calculate the forecast error as mape(val.pax, val.y_hat_lm):

```
target = y.copy()

for date in val.index:

    # build target time series using previously forecast value
    new_point = fcasted_values[-1] if len(fcasted_values) > 0 else 0.0
    target = target.append(pd.Series(index=[date], data=new_point))

    # build feature vector using previous forecast values
    features, _ = create_features(target, lags)

    new_X = pd.DataFrame(features)

    new_X.loc[:,'month'] = new_X.index.month
```

(continued)

```
    new_X = pd.get_dummies(new_X, columns=['month'], drop_first=True,
prefix='month')
    new_X.tail()

    # forecast
    predictions = lm.predict(new_X.iloc[-1:])
    fcasted_values.append(predictions[-1])

    val.loc[:,'y_hat_lm'] = pd.Series(index=val.index,
    data=fcasted_values)
```

Note that we did not use a "plain" linear regression model, but applied recursive feature elimination (RFE) with 8 parameters. Therefore, only the 8 most important features are used in the final model. Features should be eliminated from models if they do not contribute enough to the prediction quality. The more features a model has, the more likely it is to overfit which as a general goal in machine learning want to avoid.

The feature elimination step can be performed using different methods and usually should also be done by incorporating the business problem knowledge by the data scientists. For the sake of brevity and illustration of our use case here, we performed a more automated feature selection procedure which resulted in the selection of 8 parameters.

This search for the hyperparameter $k = 8$ is implemented by iterating over all possible values, i.e. 1 through the maximum number of features, fitting a linear regression model with RFE and the current hyperparameter value in the iteration, and then evaluating this fitted model on the validation set to derive the forecast error:

```
from sklearn.linear_model import LinearRegression
from sklearn.feature_selection import RFE

scores = []

for k in range(1, X.shape[1] + 1):
    model = LinearRegression()
    lm = RFE(model, k)
    lm.fit(X,y)

    fcasted_values = []
    target = y.copy()

    for date in val.index:
```

(continued)

```
            # build target time series using previously forecast value
            new_point = fcasted_values[-1] if len(fcasted_values) > 0 else 0.0
            target = target.append(pd.Series(index=[date], data=new_point))

            # build feature vector using previous forecast values
            features, _ = create_features(target, lags)

            new_X = pd.DataFrame(features)

            new_X.loc[:,'month'] = new_X.index.month
            new_X = pd.get_dummies(new_X, columns=['month'],
    drop_first=True, prefix='month')
            new_X.tail()

            # forecast
            predictions = lm.predict(new_X.iloc[-1:])
            fcasted_values.append(predictions[-1])

        val.loc[:,'y_hat_lm'] = pd.Series(index=val.index,
    data=fcasted_values)
        scores.append(mape(val.pax, val.y_hat_lm))

    plt.figure(figsize=(8, 6))
    plt.ylim(0.0,0.2)
    plt.plot(scores)
```

We can subsequently plot the forecasting error on the validation set as a function of the chose number of features in the RFE (Fig. 7.10).

The reader can see from this depiction that the forecasting error gradually decreases with increasing k until it plateaus and steeply increases again thereafter. We, therefore, choose the smallest value of k that provides us with the best forecasting performance, hence k = 8. (Note that we only evaluated the last of our folds in the hyperparameter search; for a more thorough evaluation, we would employ RFE with cross-validation where the same calculation is performed for all folds.)

A quick glance shows that the forecasting error of the resulting linear regression model has improved for our last validation set (Fig. 7.11).

Ensemble of the Linear Regression and Seasonal Naïve Models

The next model class we implemented for comparison is a simple ensemble of the linear regression and seasonal naïve models. Both models perform quite well but with different approaches, therefore it might improve our forecasting performance if we simultaneously forecast using both models and create a weighted combined forecast:

7.4 Data Science—Revenue Management Use Cases

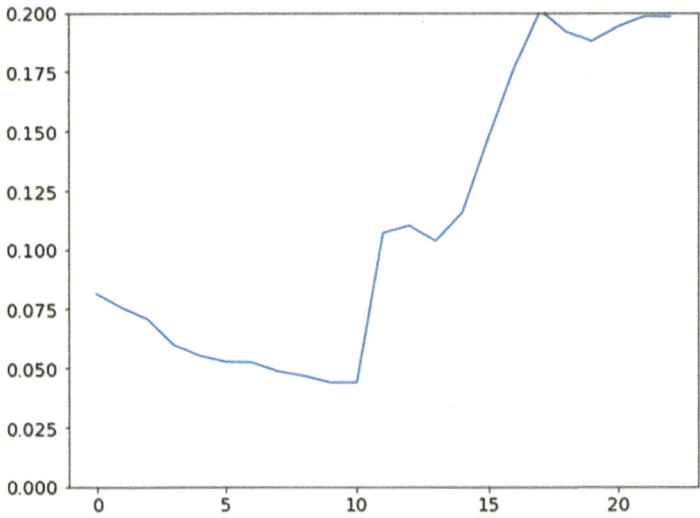

Fig. 7.10 Forecast error (MAPE) as a function of the number of features k in a linear regression model with RFE(k)

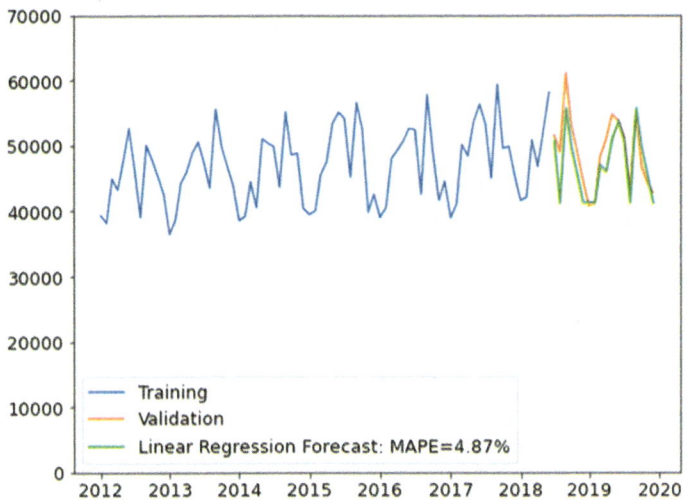

Fig. 7.11 Forecasting performance of the linear regression model with RFE

```
val.loc[:,'y_hat_ensemble'] = 0.8 * val.loc[:,'y_hat_lm'] + 0.2 * val.
loc[:,'y_hat_snaive']
```

Our resulting forecast closely follows the actual values in the validation set of the last fold (Fig. 7.12):

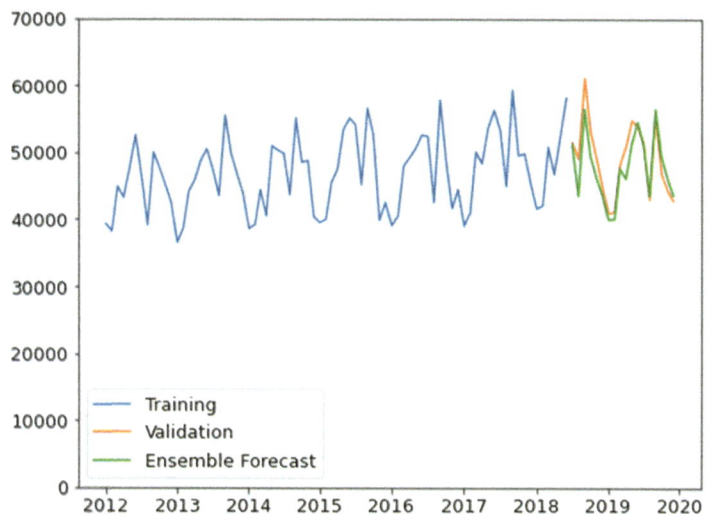

Fig. 7.12 Forecasting performance of the ensemble model

Gradient Boosting

Next, we implemented two gradient boosting models, i.e. an XGBoost and a LightGBM regression model. Gradient boosting models are quite commonly used for forecasting problems in practice as they have the following beneficial properties when compared to other models:

- Ability to generalize for high-dimensional problems
- Simple implementation compared to e.g. neural network models
- Comparably low computational cost

By virtue of the scikit-learn package, both boosting models have the same interface as the linear regression model and are instantiated as follows:

```
import xgboost as xgb
lm = xgb.XGBRegressor(objective ='reg:linear', max_depth=6,
n_estimators = 100)

from lightgbm import LGBMRegressor
lm = LGBMRegressor()
```

Fitting and forecasting are invoked with same methods, .fit() and .predict(), respectively. When we evaluate the gradient boosting models over the folds, we can see that their forecasting performance does not exceed that of the ensemble model, and we, therefore, did not pursue them any further.

7.4 Data Science—Revenue Management Use Cases

Neural Network

Lastly, we implemented a type of neural network specifically designed for sequential data like time series, a long short-term memory network or LSTM.

Neural networks require an additional data transformation step since they do not converge well during training if the input values for each feature are not from a $[-1, 1]$ interval. There are pre-defined functions to help with this step:

```
from sklearn.preprocessing import MinMaxScaler
scaler = MinMaxScaler()
scaler.fit(train)
scaled_train = scaler.transform(train)
scaled_val = scaler.transform(val)
```

For defining and training the neural network, we use the popular package Keras which has a clean and easy-to-understand API:

```
from keras.preprocessing.sequence import TimeseriesGenerator
from keras.models import Sequential
from keras.layers import Dense, LSTM, Dropout

dropout_rate = 0.0
n_neurons = [1,2,3,4,5,6,7,8,16,32,64,128]

k = 0
mape_n_neurons = np.zeros(len(n_neurons))

for n in n_neurons:
    ts_gen = TimeseriesGenerator(scaled_train, scaled_train, length=12, batch_size=1)

    model = Sequential()
    model.add(LSTM(n, input_shape= (12, 1), return_sequences=True, dropout=dropout_rate, recurrent_dropout=dropout_rate))
    model.add(LSTM(n, return_sequences=True, dropout=dropout_rate, recurrent_dropout=dropout_rate))
    model.add(LSTM(n, dropout=dropout_rate, recurrent_dropout=dropout_rate))
    model.add(Dense(1))
    model.compile(optimizer='adam', loss='mse')
```

(continued)

```
model.fit(ts_gen,verbose=2, epochs=40)

test_predictions = []
first_eval_batch = scaled_train[-12:]
current_batch = first_eval_batch.reshape((1,12,1))

for i in range(len(val)):
    current_pred = model.predict(current_batch)[0]
    test_predictions.append(current_pred)
    current_batch = np.append(current_batch[:,1:,:],
[[current_pred]], axis= 1)

true_predictions = scaler.inverse_transform(test_predictions)
val = val.copy()
val.loc[:,"y_hat"] = true_predictions

mape_n_neurons[k] = mape(val.pax, val.y_hat)
k = k+1
```

In the main loop, we are varying the capacity of the neural network, i.e. its number of neurons, as a hyperparameter. Because of their high generalization capacity, neural networks are prone to overfitting and we have to take special care to avoid this. For each possible value of the hyperparameter ([1,2,3,4,5,6,7,8,16,32,64,128]), we are fitting an LSTM and calculate the forecast error on the validation set. The following plot shows how the forecast error behaves as a function of the network capacity (Fig. 7.13):

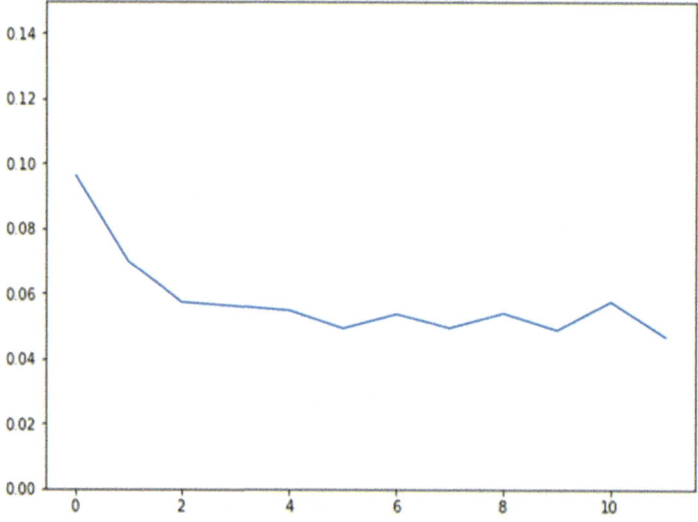

Fig. 7.13 Forecasting performance (MAPE) as a function of the network capacity

When evaluating and further adjusting the LSTM model, we find that its forecasting performance stays around c. 6% MAPE. Therefore, we also decided not to pursue this model any further.

7.4.1.6 Results and Discussion

Over the course of this section, the reader has seen how we sequentially developed five model types in the order of increasing complexity. To briefly recapitulate, these were:

- (Seasonal) naïve forecasting to set an expectation of the baseline metric
- Linear regression with recursive feature elimination (RFE)
- An ensemble of the linear regression and seasonal naïve models
- Gradient boosting, i.e., XGBoost and LightGBM
- Long short-term memory (LSTM), i.e., a neural network

We eliminated the gradient boosting and LSTM models since they did not yield a better forecasting performance and the effort for further trying to improve likely was not worth it.

Hence, for our final selection of a model, we are looking at the comparison between seasonal naïve forecasting and the ensemble model (since it includes the linear regression model) (Figs. 7.14 and 7.15).

When comparing the box plots of the respective forecasting errors across the same folds in our time series, we are able to derive three conclusions:

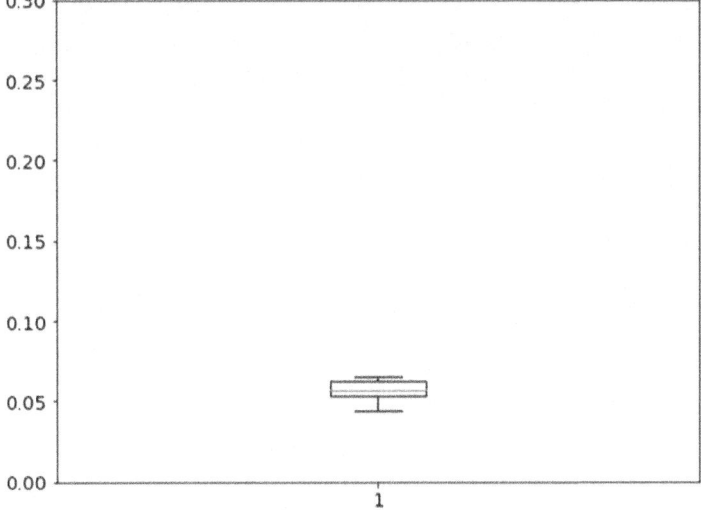

Fig. 7.14 Seasonal naive forecasting error (MAPE)

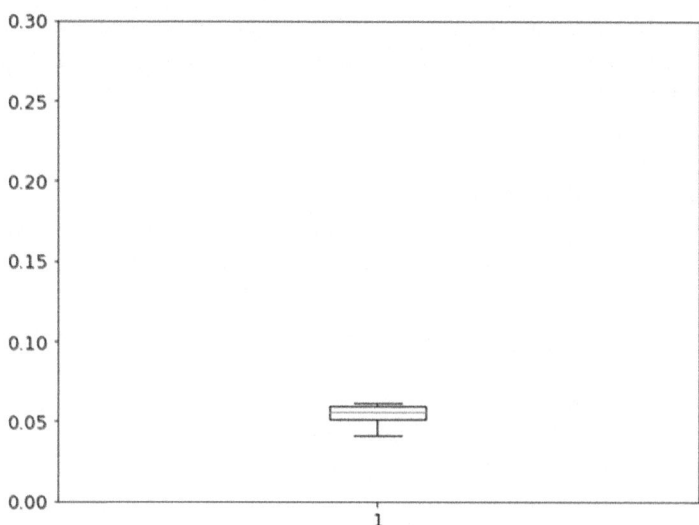

Fig. 7.15 Ensemble forecasting error (MAPE)

- The median forecasting error of the ensemble model is slightly smaller than that of the seasonal naïve forecasting model.
- The forecasting error distribution of the ensemble model is slightly more skewed toward lower errors than the seasonal naïve model.
- Both models are not able to exactly meet our forecasting goal of 5% error.

In practice, we would now weigh the cost of implementing one model over the other against the business impact of the slightly smaller forecasting error.

This use case bears an important lesson for practical business applications: it pays to work from simple approaches to more complicated ones. Not only do they provide good baselines to compare against, but often the additional quality improvement diminishes with an increasing degree of complication, therefore providing pragmatic ways of concluding a project when the result is "good enough." This principle is also known as "Occam's razor."

For forecasting specifically, the level of (temporal and/or, e.g., spatial) aggregation of the time series often determines how complicated the forecasting models need to be. As a rule of thumb, the higher the level of aggregation, the less variance there is in the time series and therefore the simpler the forecast—and vice versa. In practice, gradient boosting models have proven to be quite versatile even for detailed forecasting levels. Neural networks like the briefly discussed LSTM can provide additional performance gains for the most detailed forecasting levels and when considering cross-time-series interaction effects.

Besides this, the use case also shows why statistics is an important skill set in addition to machine learning: Model errors need to be considered as random variables and therefore, we have to evaluate and compare their distributional characteristics when judging model performance. If we would have looked at the forecasting error of only one time series fold, we would have arrived at different and wrong conclusions.

7.4.2 Data Science: Use Case—Overbooking

We stated before that data science does not only consist of machine learning, but of other methodologies as well. To give the reader an insight into a practical problem to which this applies, we consider the case of overbooking.

In this section, we will discuss the general characteristics and approach for the problem along with the use case framework used in the last section. For a detailed worked example (including code and results), we refer the reader to the concise article "Monte Carlo simulation of airline overbooking" by Mira Khare, Melanie Huynh, Arni Sturluson, and Cory Simon, https://simonensemble.github.io/2018-07/airline-overbooking.html (accessed January 23rd, 2021).

7.4.2.1 Business Problem
An airline has to decide in advance how many reservations it will accept for a given flight. It wants to maximize revenue by having each seat booked. However, passengers do not show up with a certain probability, and depending on their booked fare, the airline may not realize the full or any revenue for those passengers. Therefore, the airline wants to accept more reservations than seats to mitigate the *no-show risk*. At the same time, it wants to avoid having to refuse passengers from boarding because it accepted too many bookings.

7.4.2.2 Data Sourcing and Structure
For this problem, we mainly need one information: the no-show probability of passengers for the flight we are interested in. The probability may vary by week or month, and it may likely vary by the type of passenger (business vs. leisure). This depends on the actual scope of the problem. In the worked example, the authors considered a general no-show probability.

7.4.2.3 Methodological Problem and Goal Definition
This is a classical *optimization problem* where we want to maximize the revenue of a flight (number of passengers booked x ticket price—number of passengers refused x compensation) by setting the overbooking limit while given a certain no-show probability.

7.4.2.4 Development of the Approach(es)
In the way the problem is formulated in the worked example, the solution can be obtained analytically by applying probability theory:

- If the no-show probability is 6.5%, the expected amount of bookings needed to fill 100 seats is 100 / (100–6.5%) = 106.95

- The revenue function increases linearly with each booking and gets penalized with each overbooking (with a penalty of 2x the fare price). The optimum reservation limit, therefore, coincides with the expected amount of bookings.

However, in the example, the authors used a *simulation approach*. Here, a large number of simulation runs (10,000) is performed for an interval of overbooking limits. In each simulation run, passengers who made a reservation do not show up with the given no-show probability. The revenue function then is calculated for each simulation run to yield the revenue distribution for each overbooking limit.

7.4.2.5 Results and Discussion

As expected, the analytical result equals the result derived from the simulations. However, in practical situations where the problem is more complicated, e.g., when dealing with multiple fare classes including different no-show policies, when no-shows are dependent on the passengers (or booking class), time of year, etc., it quickly becomes infeasible to formulate and derive an analytical solution. Simulation is a handy approach for getting insights into problems. Often, simulations can be made by "replaying" historical data in different ways, an approach called bootstrapping.

In both cases, we relied on linear optimization where we could formulate the target function (revenue) to maximize. Like briefly outlined before, many practical data science problems are a combination of some other methodology and optimization in order to derive business decisions. We therefore highly recommend Operations Research as an additional skillset to any business-oriented data science function.

7.5 Data Science—An Annotated Bibliography

We mentioned the widespread availability of information and open-source code as one of the key drivers benefitting the current interest and advancement of data science. Alas, this also can make it hard for beginners to navigate the field and to choose good resources to learn from.

Therefore, in this part, we provide the reader with a set of references that in our experience are particularly helpful in creating a solid foundation for understanding, defining, and solving data science problems. You may consider us "old-fashioned," but we exclusively focused on books. There are many excellent video courses available on the internet, but in our experience, studying (and pondering) the materials in a well-structured textbook creates the best foundation for deep understanding.

Also note that our resource list focuses on data science; there are equally as many books on data engineering aspects (sourcing data from databases, storing and processing "big" data, using cloud platforms, deploying and maintaining data science applications in production) which are more relevant for the IT part, less the business part of data science applications.

We categorized the resources into three groups:

1. Theory—Covering the fundamentals of statistics, linear algebra, and machine learning. We cannot stress the importance of developing a good understanding and intuition of these enough. Only focusing on how to write code will ultimately leave you unable to solve problems that are not published anywhere—and many real-world problems in your business will not be.
2. Practical—Having understood the basics, the resources will provide the reader with the necessary tools to prototype and develop data science applications. Also, they will show how to approach many examples from different problem domains (i.e., working with tabular data, text, images, sequences, etc.).
3. Applied—There are few resources showing how the methodologies and tools are applied to actual business problems, and we have included those that are most valuable to learn.

7.5.1 Theory

- Fahrmeir et al., Statistik—Der Weg zur Datenanalyse (2016). A classical textbook covering all necessary basics of probability theory, statistical testing, and regression analysis.
- Field et al., Discovering Statistics using R (2012). Through explanation of statistical basics, interwoven with an introduction to the R statistical programming language, which can be helpful for those who start fresh in both.
- Venables/Ripley, Modern Applied Statistics with S-PLUS (1997). The S-PLUS environment predates the R statistical programming language but is very similar to it. This classical textbook provides a thorough introduction to the S-PLUS language and how to apply it to statistical problems. It is suitable for advanced readers that are also able to abstract away the programming language differences. We included it in the list because of its accessibility and depth.
- Strang, Linear Algebra and Learning from Data (2019). Linear algebra is a fundamental mathematical field data scientists need to know if they want to understand how machine learning algorithms work. This is for anyone who wants to get better at formulating machine learning problems instead of "blindly" trying libraries. Prof. Strang is a reputable teacher for the sometimes unnecessarily intimidating concepts of linear algebra.
- Abu-Mostafa et al., Learning from Data (2012). A compact and accessible course for beginners that gives a visual and solid introduction into the mathematical basics of machine learning and demonstrates how different types of machine learning algorithms work. Highly recommended for a first exposure toward machine learning theory.

- James/Witten/Hastie/Tibshirani, An Introduction to Statistical Learning: with Applications in R (2013). Also known as "the ISLR book," this is the single best resource for readers with a statistics background moving into machine learning.
- Deisenroth et al., Mathematics for Machine Learning (2020). For anyone coming from a computer science or engineering background, this book thoroughly explains the basic mathematical foundations of machine learning algorithms, i.e., how problems are described in linear algebra, how learning relates to probability and statistics, and how optimization is used to train the algorithms. It is a very good addition to more classical, statistics-focused books.
- Bishop, Pattern Recognition and Machine Learning (PRML) (2006). Another classic, a self-contained extensive course on machine learning fundamentals.
- Goodfellow/Bengio/Courville, Deep Learning (2016). A more advanced book that explains various neural network architectures as well as practical methodologies which led to the "deep learning revolution." Highly recommended for its systematic overview and accessibility.
- Barber, Bayesian Reasoning and Machine Learning (2012). The recommended first book for readers interested in approaching machine learning from a more probabilistic instead of purely mathematical perspective.
- Murphy, Machine Learning: A Probabilistic Perspective (2012). In a similar vein, this book provides a theoretical introduction to machine learning algorithms from a probabilistic view.
- Gelman, Bayesian Data Analysis (1995). A more advanced book on probabilistic models for data analysis.

7.5.2 Practical

- Downey, Think Stats (2014) and Think Bayes (2013). Two entry-level books for learning how to analyze statistical and probabilistic problems with Python. Very intuitive style built upon many practical examples.
- Grus, Data Science from Scratch (2nd edition, 2019). If you only have time to read one book that provides a (light) theoretical introduction, a programming course, and all of this explained along with practical examples, e.g., in the context of web applications, this is the book to get.
- Conway et al., Machine Learning for Hackers (2012). For readers coming from a development/coding background who would like to understand how to program basic machine learning applications, this is a good introductory resource.
- Segaran, Programming Collective Intelligence (2007). An older book, but still a good resource to get a first exposure to implementing machine learning problems in the context of web applications. A good introductory read for readers coming, e.g., from an e-commerce background.

- Géron, Hands-On Machine Learning with Scikit-Learn and TensorFlow (2nd edition, 2019). The best book for getting a full overview of the Python ecosystem for machine learning, both focusing on "classical" machine learning problems and modern deep learning techniques.
- Chollet, Deep Learning in Python (2017). A very intuitive introduction into the Python library Keras, now integrated in Tensorflow, which provides a high-level interface for describing and constructing deep learning problems. Highly recommended since it lets the reader focus on the essentials of the problems.
- Stevens et al., Deep Learning with PyTorch (2020). While carrying PyTorch in the title, which is another deep learning library competing with e.g. Keras, the reader can safely ignore this to find a very accessible, practical, and intuitive introduction into various deep learning applications. If you want to branch out into deep learning without spending time on theory or programming details, we highly recommend this book.

7.5.3 Applied

- Hillier/Lieberman, Introduction to Operations Research (2004). An older textbook, but full of practical examples of how to apply operations research methods to business problems.
- Kuhn/Johnson, Applied Predictive Modeling (2013). An excellent book showing how to deal with machine learning modeling in practice, e.g., cleaning data, dealing with data imbalances, evaluating performance, etc.
- Shmueli, Practical Time Series Forecasting: A Hands-On Guide (2011). A concise guide to various forecasting approaches explained in the context of actual business problems.
- Hyndman et al., Forecasting: Principles and Practice (2018). An extensive practical guide to both basic and advanced forecasting methods. Highly recommended as a resource for reference.
- Nielsen, Practical Time Series Analysis (2019). Practical guide to time series analysis, covering various forecasting methods, but also practical aspects e.g. of programming the analyses, acquiring and storing time series data.

7.6 Checkpoint Chap. 7

In this chapter, we provided an introduction to the key terms and methods behind modern data science. We particularly explained which mathematical foundations are necessary for a broad range of use cases and how these methods should be applied in practice. The main concepts in this chapter were:

- Model-based analytics
- Modern analytical methods (statistics, operations research, machine learning)

- Solving business problems through the analytical cycle
- "Big data" systems and data engineering
- Managing analytical capabilities in a corporate context
- Full description of a practical use case

The reader should now be able to answer the following questions:

1. Why and how is "data science" more than visualizing data?
2. What are the main success factors and pitfalls when approaching a data science project?
3. Is it necessary to have large amounts of data to initiate a data science project?
4. Is "data science" equivalent to "machine learning" and if not, which other disciplines are relevant as well and why?
5. How do you set up a data science function and team in your company?

Bibliography

Air Berlin PLC (2016). *Air Berlin—Geschäftsbericht 2016*, Statista, https://de.statista.com/statistik/daten/studie/445053/umfrage/air-berlin-kosten-je-ask/.

Belobaba, P., A. Odoni and C. Barnhart (2016). *The Global Airline Industry: Vol. Second Edition*, Wiley.

IATA (2013). *Profitability and the air transport value chain*, IATA Economics Briefing No. 10.

IATA (2016). *Another Strong Year for Airline Profits in 2017*, Press Release No: 76, online URL https://www.iata.org/en/pressroom/pr/2016-12-08-01/.

Klein, R. and C. Steinhardt (2008). *Revenue Management*, Springer-Verlag, Heidelberg.

McGill, J. I. (1995). *Censored regression analysis of multiclass demand data subject to joint capacity constraints*, Annals of Operations Research, 60:209–240.

Littlewood, K. (1972). *Forecasting and control of passenger bookings*, Proceedings of the Twelfth Annual AGIFORS Symposium, Nathanya, Israel.

Office of Aviation Enforcement and Proceedings (2019), *Air Travel Consumer Report*, December.

Poelt, S. (1998). *Forecasting is difficult—especially if it refers to the future*, Reservations and Yield Management Study Group Annual Meeting Proceedings, Melbourne, Australia, AGIFORS.

Pompl, W. (2007). *Luftverkehr*, Springer-Verlag, Heidelberg.

Statista (2019a). *Low cost carriers' worldwide market share from 2007 to 2019*, online URL https://www-statista-com.pxz.iubh.de:8443/statistics/586677/global-low-cost-carrier-market-capacity-share/.

Statista (2019b). *Survey: What would you rank as most important consideration before buying an airline ticket for personal travel?*, online URL https://www-statista-com.pxz.iubh.de:8443/statistics/1017342/us-air-travel-important-aspects-booking-personal-travel/

Talluri, K. and G. J. van Ryzin (2005). *The Theory and Practice of Revenue Management*, Springer Science + Business Media, Inc. New York.

The manufacturer's authorised representative in the EU is Springer Nature Customer Service Centre GmbH, Europaplatz 3, 69115 Heidelberg, Germany. If you have any concerns regarding our products, please contact ProductSafety@springernature.com

Printed and bound by CPI Group (UK) Ltd, Croydon, CR0 4YY

18/02/2026

02055608-0001